Invitation to live

Invitation to live

**An up-to-date version
of a timeless classic
by
Richard Baxter**

John Blanchard

 EVANGELICAL PRESS

EVANGELICAL PRESS
12 Wooler Street, Darlington, Co. Durham, DL1 1RQ, England

© Evangelical Press 1991
First published 1991

British Library Cataloguing in Publication Data Available

ISBN 0 85234 285 3

Other books by John Blanchard

Gathered Gold
How to Enjoy your Bible
Luke Comes Alive!
More Gathered Gold
Pop Goes the Gospel
Read Mark Learn
Right With God
Training for Triumph
Truth for Life
Ultimate Questions
What in the World is a Christian?
Will the Real Jesus Please Stand Up?

Printed in Great Britain by the Bath Press, Avon.

Contents

Preface

Richard Baxter was a household name in England towards the end of the seventeenth century. An influential army chaplain during the Civil War, actively involved in the country's ecclesiastical and political life (he was prepared at times to stand up to Oliver Cromwell), chaplain to Charles II, influential in the overthrow of James II and invited to become Bishop of Bedford (an offer he turned down), Baxter moved in some pretty lofty circles.

Yet he was not a politician, but a pastor, and his greatest achievement was not on a national scale, but on a local one. In 1641 he was appointed vicar of Kidderminster, in Worcestershire, which then had a population of around 2,000. When he began his ministry there, he found 'an ignorant, rude and revelling people'.[1] In some streets not more than one family went to church. As well as preaching on Sunday and Thursday (an hour each time!), Baxter began a relentless programme of visitation, personal counselling and teaching, visiting home after home, time after time. Gradually, a remarkable change came over the whole town, so that by the time he left, twenty years later, it was difficult to find one family in a street that had not been spiritually transformed. On most Sundays 1,000 people crammed into the church (five galleries had to be built to accommodate them). Six years after he left, he had not heard of a single convert who had fallen away. Baxter's work at Kidderminster remains one of the most amazing pastoral achievements in English church history.

Somehow, he found time to be a prolific author, with nearly 150 publications to his name. He is best known for three books in particular. The first of these, *The Saints' Everlasting Rest*, first published in 1650, is a book about heaven, and recognized as a classic on the subject. The second was *The Reformed Pastor*, first published in 1656, and perhaps the most challenging book ever written exclusively to pastors.

Baxter's third great book, written at the suggestion of James Ussher, Archbishop of Armagh, was *A Call to the Unconverted*, first published in 1658, and regarded by many as the greatest book on Christian conversion that has ever been written. Within a year there were at least 20,000 copies in print. Every week he received letters telling of the remarkable way in which God was using the book, not only in English but in several foreign translations. He once heard of six brothers converted through reading it, and it is thought to have been used to the conversion of thousands. No wonder it was said at his funeral that the book spoke with great authority and would be powerfully effective 'while the church remained on earth'.[2]

In the last 300 years (Baxter died on 8 December 1691) *A Call to the Unconverted* has been reprinted many times, most recently by Evangelical Press in 1976, but as far as I know nobody has revised and updated the book to make it more easily readable (and therefore more understandable and useful) as we approach the beginning of the twenty-first century. This is what I have attempted to do.

Firstly, the book has been shortened a little by tightening the style and reworking virtually every sentence. Like most of his fellow Puritans, Baxter was inclined to be very repetitive. I have tried to reduce this, but not to eliminate it, because it reveals something of Baxter's heart as well as his mind. He is passionately concerned that his readers hear what he is saying — and that they do something about it. At other times, I have taken the liberty of inserting material where I felt this would provide better linkage in the argument. I have, however, done some major surgery to the introduction, which originally ran to something over twenty-five pages, as most of what Baxter wrote there is repeated in the body of the book. This has given me room to insert an introduction to the passage from the Bible on which the whole book is based. I have also given the book a shorter, more positive title.

Secondly, I have redistributed the material. For example, in Baxter's version, the first chapter runs to over thirty pages, while the next has just seven.

Thirdly, I have sub-divided the chapters into bite-sized sections, again to make the book more easily digestible.

Fourthly, I have modernized the language. One example will serve as an illustration. At one point in his introduction Baxter writes of '...a thief that sits merrily spending the money in an ale-house which he hath stolen, when men are riding in post-haste to apprehend him'. This has been changed to '...a thief sitting in a bar celebrating his latest haul, little knowing that the police are just around the corner and on their way to arrest him'.

Fifthly, I have recast the entire book in the second person singular. It is now addressed to 'you', and not to 'us' or 'them'. Baxter's original work switched in and out of all three classes of personal pronouns — there are times when he almost seemed to be addressing a congregation — but this is such an intensely personal book that I have worked it all into the form which I believe is best suited to its message.

Finally, almost all Bible quotations are from the New International Version, one of the finest modern translations now available. Some are from the New King James Version, which is another excellent modern translation and which closely relates to the Authorized (or King James) Version, which Baxter used.

For all of these changes, the book remains essentially the same. The original author is from the seventeenth century and the present one from the twentieth, but the message is timeless. The book sits the reader down, looks him right in the eye, pleads with him to be ruthlessly honest in examining his own spiritual condition, and urges him to turn to God in repentance and faith in order that he might receive the forgiveness of sins and eternal life. It also leaves the reader in no doubt about the alternative!

The message comes from God.
The response must come from you.

JOHN BLANCHARD
Banstead
Surrey
March 1991

1. *Reliquiae Baxterianae*
2. By Dr William Bates

Introduction

I am writing these pages as one seeking to obey God's voice and to fulfil the tremendous responsibility he has placed upon me and upon all true ministers of the gospel. We have been commanded to preach the Word of God 'in season and out of season' and to 'correct, rebuke and encourage — with great patience and careful instruction' (2 Timothy 4:2).

We have a terrible and difficult task. We are charged first of all with telling men of their transgressions and sins and of the danger they are in as a result of these — and to keep on doing so even if we are rejected and our hearts are broken by those whose hearts are hardened. There are times when we feel helpless and hopeless in the face of our task. We try to make things clear, and many refuse to understand; we try to arouse men's consciences, and they feel nothing; we seek to be serious, and they ignore us; we try to reason with them, but they will not listen to reason; we argue from the Word of God, and they shut their ears. What can we do to help those who refuse to be helped? We can do nothing more than to bring the

same message to them in God's name, as I shall seek to do in
the following pages.

But we also have a glorious task. We are to announce that
the God who created man loves him in spite of his rebellion
and sin, and that in the life, death and resurrection of his only
Son, the Lord Jesus Christ, he has provided a way of salvation
by which man can receive the forgiveness of sins and eternal
life. God no longer speaks to men by prophets and apostles,
who received their message by direct revelation; instead, he
has appointed faithful ministers to preach the same gospel
which Christ and his apostles delivered. Yet even when we
preach such a glorious message we are rejected by many. The
gospel is turned aside; heaven has no appeal and hell holds no
fear. What can we do for men who treat the Word of God in
such a way? We can do nothing more than repeat the message,
and plead with them to accept it.

Where do you stand in all of this? What part does God play
in your life? In which direction is your life facing? Are you
taken up with your earthly possessions and position? Are you
spending your life drowning your conscience in self-satisfy-
ing pleasure, without any concern as to whether you are
pleasing God? Do you never stop to think about your *soul*? Do
you never stop to ask whether you are ready to appear before
God on the Day of Judgement? Have you never realized that
God is keeping a full and infallible record of your sins, and that
one day you will give an account of them to him? And do you
realize that on the Day of Judgement all who are not right with
God 'will go away to eternal punishment'? (Matthew 25:46).
Your life is going and death is coming; and when death comes
there will be no time to change your mind or amend your ways.
You are only a heart-beat away from death, judgement and
condemnation. A few more days, a bit more fun, a few more
honours or riches or pleasures or possessions and all of these

will be over. You will then stand naked before God, with not a word to say in your defence. You are like a thief sitting in a bar celebrating his latest haul, little knowing that the police are just around the corner and on their way to arrest him.

If only you would listen to what I have to say! If only you would understand the greatness of God's love and the riches he offers you in the gospel! If only you knew what it was to have your sins forgiven and to have eternal life! If you did, you would fling away your sins, change the whole course of your life, and turn your affections and actions in a totally different direction. You would be a changed person!

Would it not be better to live with the assurance of having your sins forgiven and of going to heaven when you die, than to live under the shadow of God's judgement? Remember, your life here on earth will not last for ever. You dare not think that you can get away with neglecting God, debasing your soul, ignoring the gospel and refusing to be changed. One day God will require you to pay a terrible price for all of these.

Some people care very little about these things because they imagine that God cares very little about them; but to think like that is to think like an atheist. Does the Creator care nothing for the one he has created? Does the One who 'gives all men life and breath and everything else' (Acts 17:25) not care whether you live or die? And if he cares for your body, surely he cares for your soul? Does the sovereign Ruler of the universe not care what happens in his world? Would God give man his holy law and then not care whether he kept it? If God did not care for man, why did he send his Son 'to be the Saviour of the world'? (1 John 4:14).

Let me put all of this to you in two other ways. Firstly, do you care what other men say about you or do to you? Does it matter to you if they abuse you, injure you, steal your goods, or destroy your property? Of course it does! Then do you imagine that God cares nothing about the way you treat him? Secondly, do you care anything about law, order or justice? Would you be perfectly happy to live in a world where there was total anarchy, where everyone was free to do exactly as he pleased — even if it meant hurting or killing you or the members of your family? Of course not! Then do you imagine that God has no standards, no laws, no justice? Do you really think that he will treat the godly and the ungodly in exactly the same way? Nothing could be further from the truth. The Bible says that 'The Lord watches over the way of the righteous, but the way of the ungodly will perish' (Psalm 1:6).

In this book, I want to focus your attention on just one verse in the Bible. It comes in the Old Testament, and was part of the message given by God to his prophet Ezekiel to deliver to the people of Israel. This is what God told him: '*Say to them, "As surely as I live, declares the Sovereign Lord, I take no pleasure in the death of the wicked, but rather that they turn from their ways and live. Turn! Turn from your evil ways! Why will you die, O house of Israel"*' (Ezekiel 33:11).

Everything I have to say in this book is based on those words, which capture exactly the spirit of the Christian gospel. In response I would ask you to do three things. Firstly, read the book slowly and seriously. Secondly, as you read it, think carefully about what you are reading. Ask God to open your eyes to see the truth of his Word and to give you all the help you need to understand and obey it. Thirdly, when you are convinced of your need and of the answer that God has provided, obey his call and turn to him with all your heart.

It may well be that many will read these pages and go on as they were before — careless, ignorant, worldly and un-godly. If that should be the case, then all I can do is remember that Christ called his people a 'little flock' (Luke 12:32) and said that 'only a few' (Matthew 7:14) would find the road that leads to life. When you have read these pages, I will be done with you. But unless you are converted sin will not be done with you, the devil will not be done with you — and God will not be done with you! Instead, you will be one of those who will be 'punished with everlasting destruction and shut out from the presence of the Lord and from the majesty of his power' (2 Thessalonians 1:9).

I write as one who will soon be in another world, and who knows that you will soon be there too. If you want to meet me in the comforting presence of our Maker, if you want to be received into God's eternal glory and to escape the everlasting torments of hell, I beg of you to hear what God is saying to you, obey his call, turn to him — and live! If you refuse, I call upon you to answer to God for your refusal, to bear me witness that I warned you, and to admit that you are to be condemned not because you were not called to turn and live, but because you were not willing to do so.

1.
The letter of the law

It would probably come as an amazing shock to you — as it once did to me — to read how few people the Bible says will go to heaven when they die. It may come as an even greater surprise — and a very sobering one — to discover that even of those who have heard the gospel most will be shut out of heaven and spend eternity in hell. Of course there are many who refuse to believe this — because they reject the Bible's teaching — but one day they will be forced to experience its truth. Those who do believe it can only cry out with one of the Bible's writers, 'Oh, the depth of the riches both of the wisdom and knowledge of God! How unsearchable are his judgements, and his ways past finding out!' (Romans 11:33, NKJV).

The thought of most of mankind spending eternity in hell immediately raises a massive question: 'Why?' Who is responsible for this appalling catastrophe? Whenever something goes wrong, we automatically want to know the reason.

In the case of something evil, our instincts for justice drive us to search for the culprit so that he can be made to bear the shame and the punishment he deserves. If we came across the body of a man who had been murdered, we would want to know who killed him. If a town was deliberately set on fire, we would want the arsonist brought to justice. So when we read of millions of souls suffering for ever in the torments of hell, surely we should be asking who is responsible? Who could be so cruel as to be the cause of such a thing? Whose fault is it?

Many people would reply that the devil is responsible, and there is a sense in which that is true, but he is not the principal cause. It is true that hell is the punishment for sin and that it is the devil who tempts people to commit sin, but he does not *compel* them to sin. Instead, he leaves it to their own will whether to resist temptation or yield to it. The devil does not carry a man to someone else's property and force him to steal it; nor does he put him under arrest every Sunday and prevent him from going to church; nor does he tear his mind away from holy thoughts. The person concerned *chooses* to act the way he does. But if the devil is not the principal cause of a person's sin, who is? There are only two possibilities — God, or the person concerned. Yet God specifically disclaims all responsibility — and sinners usually do so too. This is the issue that I am going to deal with in examining the words recorded by Ezekiel.

Is God guilty?

This very argument — God saying that the people are at fault and the people saying that God is to blame — surfaced earlier in Ezekiel when the people complained, 'The way of the Lord is not just' (Ezekiel 18:25). Here they said much the same thing: 'Our offences and sins weigh us down, and we are wasting away because of them. How then can we live?' (Ezekiel 33:10). In effect they were saying, 'If sins are ruining our lives, and damning us for eternity, how can we be to blame? Surely God must be responsible?' But God makes it clear that he is *not* responsible. What is more, he shows them how to use the means he has provided for them to be saved from their terrible situation. But he also tells them that if they refuse to do what he says it will be their own fault, and he will not hesitate to judge and punish them. On the other hand, they have neither the authority, the wisdom nor the impartiality to judge themselves, let alone God. What is more, quarrelling with God and quibbling at what he does will do nothing to save them from the execution of his justice. In the words of the verse we are going to examine, God does two things.

Firstly, he clears himself from any blame with regard to the eternal destruction of the wicked. He does this, not by disowning his law, which says that the wicked *will* be destroyed, nor by evading responsibility for the execution of his law, nor by giving sinners any hope that his law will not be executed. Instead, he makes it clear that his pleasure lies not in their destruction but in their turning to him in order that they might have eternal life.

Secondly, he not only expressly commands the wicked to turn to him, but even condescends to reason through the issue with them. He does this in order to convince them that he is not at fault and that by rejecting all his commands and efforts they themselves are to blame. In other words, God tells them that if sinners die in their sins it is because they are determined to do so.

That is the broad outline of what God is saying in this verse, which forms the basis of this book. When we look at it in more detail, we discover at least seven great truths or principles.

1. It is an unchangeable law of God that the wicked must turn from their wickedness or they will be damned.

2. God promises that if the wicked will turn, they will receive eternal life.

3. God takes pleasure in men's conversion and salvation, not in their death or damnation; he had rather they would turn to him and live than go on in their wickedness and die.

4. God is so concerned that men should not question these truths that he solemnly confirms them with an oath.

5. God is so zealous for the conversion of sinners that he repeats and emphasizes his commands and persuasions to them to turn to him and live.

6. God condescends to reason the case with the wicked; he asks them, 'Why will you die?'

7. If, after all this, the wicked refuse to turn, it is not God's fault if they perish; it is theirs. Their own wilfulness is the cause of their own damnation; they are damned because they choose to be.

These seven great truths or principles will be highlighted in turn as we examine in detail God's statement to the prophet Ezekiel. They are principles that remain as firm now as they were when God first spoke those words to his servant.

The Bible tells us so

The first of these seven great principles is this: *it is an unchangeable law of God that the wicked must turn from their wickedness or they will be condemned for ever.*

The Word of God makes it crystal clear that the sinner has one of two options: conversion or condemnation. Many people find it difficult to believe that this is either true or fair, but it is hardly surprising that sinners quarrel with God's law. Not many people are inclined to believe something they would rather not be true; even fewer want something to be true if it is to their disadvantage.

But quarrelling with the law will not save the criminal. If this were not the case, for every man who would sensibly submit to the law, a hundred would argue with it. Men would sooner give reasons why they should not be punished than listen to the reasons and decisions of those responsible for administering the law. But laws are made to rule and judge, not to be ruled and judged. That being the case, is there anyone so blind as to question either the truth or the justice of this law of God — that the wicked must turn from their wickedness or they will be condemned? Let me give you evidence of both its truth and its justice.

Firstly, if you doubt whether this *is* the law of God, here are a few of several hundred statements from the Bible that should make it clear that it is.

Jesus said, 'Unless you are converted and become as little children, you will by no means enter the kingdom of heaven' (Matthew 18:3, NKJV). On another occasion he said, 'I tell you the truth, no one can see the kingdom of God unless he is born again' (John 3:3). One New Testament writer said, 'Make every effort ... to be holy; without holiness no one will see the Lord' (Hebrews 12:14), while another wrote, 'Those controlled by the sinful nature cannot please God' (Romans 8:8). These all confirm statements like this one in the Old Testament: 'The Lord examines the righteous, but the wicked and those who love violence his soul hates' (Psalm 11:5).

These words are so plain that they need no explanation. Nor do I need to quote any others which say the same thing. If you believe the Bible is the Word of God, here is enough evidence to convince you that the wicked must be converted or condemned. If you deny the truth of these statements you are refusing to believe what God has said — and if that is the case there is little hope for you; you are already on your way to hell.

Does that sound too harsh? But surely there is no alternative if you call God a liar? What is more, if you look God in the face and call him a liar you can hardly blame him if he gives you no further warnings but abandons you as hopeless. Why should God go on warning you if you stubbornly refuse to believe him? Presumably you would not believe if God should send an angel from heaven to speak to you. After all, an angel can only speak the Word of God — we are specifically told that if any man or angel preaches anything other than God's Word, he is to be 'eternally condemned' (Galatians 1:8) — yet surely no angel is to be believed before the Son of God, the Lord Jesus Christ, who came from heaven and brought God's truth to us? If Jesus is not to be believed, then all the angels in heaven are not to be believed. And if that is where you stand, God will one day make you hear in a more convincing way. He *pleads* with you to hear the voice of his gospel, but he will *force* you to hear the voice of his judgement. Nothing I can say will make you believe God's Word against your will, but if you refuse to do so God will one day make you suffer against your will.

Dangerous delusion

But why should you not believe the Word of God which tells you that the wicked must be converted or condemned? I know why! It is because you think it unlikely that God would say such a thing. You think it would be cruel to damn men everlastingly for a few years of sinful living. But you are wrong! The Bible says of God that 'Everything he does is right and all his ways are just' (Daniel 4:37).

Secondly, this leads us to see that God is perfectly just in condemning sinners. Surely you will not deny that man's immortal soul should be governed by laws that promise either an immortal reward or endless punishment? If this were not the case (in other words, if the laws governing the souls of men only dealt in temporary issues) they would not be suitable. Our souls are immortal and they must be governed by laws that deal in terms of eternity, not merely in terms of time. When laws concerning very serious criminal offences prescribe penalties of, say, 100 years in prison, they would be suitable in the sense that they cover the whole of a human life-span; but if man lived to be 800 or 900 years of age they would not be suitable, because a convicted criminal could serve his sentence in full and then enjoy hundreds of years of life unpunished. Exactly the same principle applies here: the laws governing eternal souls must deal in eternal terms. Men are happy to agree that God's promise of heaven speaks of something that is endless; why should they doubt that his warning about hell speaks about something that is equally endless? When you read in God's Word that this is so, do you think you are qualified to disagree? Are you prepared to accuse your Maker of lying? Are you so conceited that you will sit in judgement on God? Are you wiser and better and more righteous than he is? Must the God of heaven come to you to get wisdom? Can the One who is infinitely wise learn from your foolishness, and the One who is infinitely pure be corrected by someone who cannot keep himself clean for an hour at a time? Must the Almighty stand to be judged by a worm? What senseless arrogance! This is like a mole, or a clod of earth, or a heap of dung, accusing

the sun of darkness and undertaking to do a better job of giving
daylight to the world!

Where were you when God made the laws by which he
governs the universe? Why did he not ask for your help?
Because he made them before you were born — and in any
case he needed no one to give him advice. You came into the
world too late to change God's laws, even if you could have
done so. Perhaps you think that if you had been alive at the time
you would have prevented Adam from the death penalty of his
sin. Perhaps you would have contradicted Moses and the other
Old Testament writers. Perhaps you would even have contradicted Jesus himself, or so arranged things that it would not
have been necessary for him to live or die here on earth. And
what if God comes to an end of his patience with you,
withdraws his sustaining power that keeps you alive, and
allows you to fall into hell while you are quarrelling with his
Word and toying with your ridiculous ideas? Will you then
believe there is a hell?

The sinfulness of sin

But there are many other biblical reasons for believing in the
reality of hell. For instance, if sin is such an evil thing that it
needed the death of Jesus Christ, the Son of God, to deal with
it, surely it deserves the eternal punishment of sinners? Again,
if, as the Bible teaches, the sins of devils deserve endless
torment, why not the sins of men? Surely you realize that it is
not possible for even the best of men to be competent judges
of the right punishment for sin? There are at least six things
you would need to know before you could fully know how evil
sin is: the true value of the soul, which sin deforms; the true
nature of holiness, which sin obliterates; the true nature and

excellence of God's law, which sin violates; the true nature of God's glory, which sin despises; the true character and purpose of reason, which sin insults; and the infinite glory, omnipotence and holiness of God, against which all sin is committed. If you begin to get a grasp of these, you will begin to get a grasp of the sinfulness of sin and the punishment it deserves.

You know perfectly well that a criminal is too biased to sit in judgement on the law, or on the proceedings of a court of law. In the same way, the sinner judges by feelings which blind his reason. Most men think that their own cause is right and that anything to their detriment is wrong, and not even the wisest or most impartial friends can persuade them otherwise. Most children think their parents are being unfair if they punish them. Most criminals would readily accuse the law or the judge of wrongdoing if that would help their cause.

But do you really think that unholy people are fit to go to heaven? After all, they are unable to love God here on earth, nor can they serve him in a way which God will accept. Instead, the whole tendency of their lives is against God; they hate what God loves and love what God hates. They can never experience the imperfect communion with God which Christians enjoy here on earth; how, then, could they possibly live in that perfect union with God which his people enjoy for ever in heaven? You would not think you were being unmerciful if you refused to take your worst enemy into your confidence, or if you refused to keep pigs in your house. Yet you are prepared to blame God, the wise, gracious and Sovereign Lord of the universe, if he condemns the unconverted to eternal misery! Instead of quarrelling with God and his Word, I beg of you to hear what it has to say and to use it for your own good! If you are unconverted, you can take this as a certainty from the Word of God: *before long you must be converted or condemned.*

When you realize that it is God, the Maker and Judge of the world, who is telling you this, surely it is time to listen? Have you begun to grasp this? You are dead and damned unless you are converted. If I were to tell you otherwise I would be lying. If I were to hide this from you, your blood would be on my hands. This is exactly what God told Ezekiel: 'When I say to the wicked, "O wicked man, you will surely die," and you do not speak out to dissuade him from his ways, that wicked man will die for his sin, and I will hold you accountable for his blood' (Ezekiel 33:8).

This may sound very harsh, but I have to say it and you have to hear it. Surely it is easier to hear about hell than to experience it? If your situation was not so serious I would not try to unsettle you with such things. But there would be fewer people in hell today if they had been willing to listen to such teaching and recognize exactly where they stood. The reason so few escape hell is because they make no attempt to go through the narrow gate of conversion and then live a life of discipline and holiness while they have the opportunity of doing so. The reason they make no effort to do so is that they are not alert to the danger they are in. And they are not alert to their danger because they are reluctant to hear about it or to give it any serious thought.

If this is true of you, if you refuse to believe these things, I think the seriousness of the subject ought to force you to consider it and to give you no peace of mind until you are converted. If you heard an angel — just once — warning you, 'You must be converted or condemned; turn or die,' would it not stick in your mind and haunt you night and day? What a happy thing it would be if that were the case and the angel's words refused to let you alone until you had got right with God! But if you are determined to forget these things, or refuse to believe them, how will you ever be converted? Yet you can be sure of this: you may be able to put this truth out of your mind, but you are not able to take it out of the Bible. 'Turn or die' is an unchangeable truth and one way or the other you will eventually experience it for ever.

Then why are sinners not struck by such an important truth? One would think that any unconverted person who heard these words would be convicted of his sin and never be at rest until he was converted — yet most remain careless and negligent. If you are one of these, let me assure you that things will change one day. Conversion or condemnation will one day awaken you. I can tell you this as surely as if I could see it with my own eyes. Either grace or hell will one day make you realize how foolish you were to reject what God was saying to you.

2.
Man unmasked

There are two particular things that help to harden the unconverted — their misunderstanding of the words 'wicked' and 'turn'. Some think, 'Even if it is true that the wicked must turn or die, this does not apply to me, because, although I am a sinner (like all other men) I am not "wicked".' Others think, 'I know we must turn from our evil ways, but I have already done this.' So wicked men refuse to admit that they are wicked, while others think they have already turned from their wickedness. Before I go any further I must therefore explain exactly who are meant by 'the wicked', who must turn or die, exactly what is meant by 'turning' and what are the signs of true conversion.

In the beginning...

To explain 'wickedness' and 'conversion' I must begin at the beginning. At creation God made three kinds of living beings.

Firstly, he made *angels*, who were created as pure spirits without bodies, and therefore were made only for heaven and not for earth. Secondly, he made *animals*, who were given bodies but not souls, and were therefore made only for earth and not for heaven. Thirdly, God created *man*, with both body and soul, and therefore made for both heaven and earth. But just as man's body is meant to serve his soul, so his time on earth is only meant to provide a way to heaven. Earth was never intended to be man's final home. Man was made for heaven, where he would live in God's glorious presence for ever, loving him and being filled with his love. What is more, when he created man God gave him the means for achieving this. Firstly, man was given as much knowledge of God as was necessary and relevant, and a heart that was naturally inclined to love and obey God. But this inclination towards God was not rigidly fixed; man was not created as a puppet. Instead, God gave him free will, the ability to choose what he would do. Secondly, God gave man his perfect law and commanded him to keep it by living a life of perfect love and obedience towards God.

But man deliberately broke God's law and in doing so he not only forfeited his hopes of eternal life; he also turned his heart from God and fixed it on earthly things, blotting out the spiritual image of God from his soul. By his deliberate sin man fell short of the glory of God (the purpose for which he was created) and turned aside from the only way to heaven. He lost his holy love for God and became infected with a love for sin and self. He became separated from God and attached to the world, and as a result his lifestyle was radically changed. Instead of living to please God, he lived from then onwards to please himself.

The fatal flaw

As a result of Adam's sin all men are born with this corrupt and sinful inclination. As the Bible puts it, 'Who can bring a clean thing out of an unclean? No one!' (Job 14:4, NKJV). Just as a lion has a fierce and cruel nature before it attacks and eats its victim, and a snake has a venomous nature before it bites anyone, so as newborn babies we had sinful inclinations before we thought, spoke or did anything that was wrong. This is the clearest possible explanation for the sinful activities that now fill our lives. What is more, although God in his mercy has provided a remedy for man's situation by sending the Lord Jesus Christ to be his Saviour and to bring him back to God, man loves his sinful state so much that he is reluctant to leave it. Even when religious tradition means that he sometimes goes through the motions of giving thanks to Christ, he refuses the claims of Christ and rejects his commands to turn from sin and to live a godly life. Make a careful note of these words. If necessary, read them again, because they are an accurate summary of your natural state. They describe what 'wicked' means; they show that *everyone* in his natural corrupted nature is wicked and in a state of spiritual death.

The meaning of conversion

Then what does it mean to be converted? Because God did not want man to perish in his sin, he provided a remedy. In the person of his eternal Son he took our human nature upon him (in other words, became a man), and then, as both God and man, became a mediator between God and men, and by dying on the cross for man's sins ransomed men from the curse of God and the power of the devil. This means that God the Father and Jesus Christ his Son have brought a new law into being. It is not like the first law, which offered eternal life only to those who were perfectly obedient (which none were) and condemned all who broke it (as everyone did). Instead, there is now what we could call 'a law of grace', a promise of forgiveness and everlasting life to all who are truly converted to God by turning from their sins and putting their trust in Christ. It is like a king offering an amnesty to any rebel who will lay down his arms and agree to be his loyal subject. But God knew that man's heart was so corrupt that left to himself he would never accept this offer, so he did something else: in the person of the Holy Spirit he inspired certain men to convey his message in the Holy Scriptures. Now, by the same Spirit, he enables sinners to understand the gospel and to respond to it.

You will see from this that each of the three persons in the Godhead — the Father, the Son and the Holy Spirit — are involved in bringing about man's salvation.

The Father created us, ruled us, gave us his law and judged us by that law; and in mercy he provided us with a Redeemer in the person of his Son Jesus Christ and accepted the ransom Christ paid by dying in the place of sinners.

The Son came to redeem sinners by living a life of perfect obedience to God's law and dying to pay its penalty; he provided and preached the promise of salvation; along with the Father he has sent the Holy Spirit into the world, and he will eventually be the Judge of all mankind on the basis of their response to his grace.

The Holy Spirit caused the Word of God to be written by inspiring and guiding the human authors of the Holy Scriptures, sometimes confirming this by giving the writers miraculous gifts; he continues to give true ministers of God's Word insight into its truth and the ability to preach it faithfully, and by that same Word he brings men to illumination and conversion. Just as we could not be rational creatures if God the Father had not created us, nor have any access to God unless God the Son had died in the place of sinners, so we can never come to trust in Christ and be saved unless the Holy Spirit enables us to do so.

Notice again how the three persons in the Godhead are involved in man's salvation. The Father sends the Son; the Son redeems and announces the 'gospel' (the good news of what he has done, the message the apostles wrote down and which true ministers of the gospel preach); and the Holy Spirit takes the faithful preaching of God's Word and makes it effective by opening the hearts of men to receive it. All of this is done to turn men's hearts from being set upon sin and self and to set their lives on the road to heaven by bringing them to trust Christ.

The sinners and the saved

You should now see what it is to be 'wicked' and what it is to be 'converted', but it may help if I gave a fuller explanation. A wicked person can be known in three ways.

Firstly, his heart is set on earth and not on heaven; he loves the creature more than God; he cares more for earthly prosperity than for eternal happiness; he loves natural things but has no appetite for spiritual things. He may agree that heaven is better than earth, but he is not seriously concerned about it; he would sooner live here than there. A life of perfect holiness in the presence of God, loving and praising him for ever in heaven, does not appeal to him as much as physical health and his earthly position and possessions. The wicked might even say that he loves God, but he has no personal experience of God's love. His mind remains set on worldly or fleshly pleasures. Put very simply, anyone who loves earth more than heaven, his possessions more than God, is unconverted — he is 'wicked'.

On the other hand, anyone who is converted understands something of the loveliness of God and is so convinced of the glory to which God has called him that his heart is more taken up with this than with anything in the world. The person who is truly converted would rather live in God's eternal presence than have all of this world's wealth or pleasures. He sees the emptiness of earthly things and realizes that only God can satisfy his soul. Whatever anyone else does, he is determined to release his hold on earthly things; his hopes and his treasures are in heaven. Just as the fire leaps upwards, and the magnetic needle points north, so the converted soul is inclined towards God. Nothing else can satisfy him, nor can he find peace of heart anywhere but in God's love. In a word, those who are converted love God more than the world, and heavenly joy more than earthly prosperity. One of the psalmists put it like this:

'Whom have I in heaven but you?
And there is none upon earth that I desire besides you.
My flesh and my heart fail;
but God is the strength of my heart and my portion for ever'
(Psalm 73:25-26, NKJV).

Jesus said, 'Do not store up for yourselves treasures on earth, where moth and rust destroy, and where thieves break in and steal. But store up for yourselves treasures in heaven, where moth and rust do not destroy, and where thieves do not break in and steal. For where your treasure is, there your heart will be also' (Matthew 6:19-21). Speaking of himself and his fellow Christians, the apostle Paul said, 'But our citizenship is in heaven' (Philippians 3:20). Elsewhere he told Christians,

'Set your minds on things above, not on earthly things' (Colossians 3:2) and that 'Those who live according to the sinful nature have their minds set on what that nature desires; but those who live in accordance with the Spirit have their minds set on what the Spirit desires' (Romans 8:5).

Secondly, the wicked man is one whose principal concern in life is to please himself. He may even have a smattering of religion, he may not commit particularly gross sins, but the fact remains that he never makes it the principal concern of his life to please God. He gives God life's left-overs, as much time or effort as he thinks he can spare. He is not prepared to give up everything for God and heaven.

On the other hand, a converted man is one who does make it the principal concern of his life to please God. All the blessings of this life he sees as helping him on his way towards another, heavenly life. He submits his whole life to God. He lives a holy life and longs to be more holy. Whatever sin he commits he hates, and longs and prays and strives to be rid of it. The whole drift and bent of his life is towards God. If he sins, it is against the general direction of his life and he regrets it and turns from it. He does not wilfully allow any sin to dominate him. There is nothing in the world so dear to him that he would not give it up and forsake it for God and for the hope of sharing his eternal glory. The Bible has a great deal to say along these lines. Jesus said, 'But seek first [God's] kingdom and his righteousness' (Matthew 6:33). The apostle Paul said that 'If by the Spirit you put to death the misdeeds of the body, you will live, because those who are led by the Spirit of God are sons of God' (Romans 8:13-14), and that 'Those who belong to Christ Jesus have crucified the sinful nature with its passions and desires' (Galatians 5:24). All of this is underlined by God's wonderful promise that 'When Christ, who is your life, appears, then you also will appear with him in glory' (Colossians 3:4).

Thirdly, the wicked man never truly understands or enjoys
what the Bible says about man's redemption; nor does he
gratefully accept God's offer of a Saviour; nor is he impressed
by Christ's love; nor is he willing to submit to Christ's
authority so that he may be saved from the guilt and power of
his sins and be made right with God. Instead, his heart is
deadened to these things — and he would prefer it that way. He
may even be willing to be outwardly religious, but he refuses
to submit to the rule of Christ, the authority of God's Word and
the directions of the Holy Spirit.

On the other hand, a converted man, knowing that his sin
has ruined him, destroyed his peace with God and wrecked his
hope of heaven, gladly welcomes the gospel and puts his trust
in the Lord Jesus Christ as his only Saviour. For the converted
man, Christ is the life of his soul. He lives by him, he turns to
him in his every need and rejoices in God's wisdom and love
in providing such a Saviour. The apostle Paul put it this way:
'I have been crucified with Christ and I no longer live, but
Christ lives in me. The life I live in the body, I live by faith in
the Son of God, who loved me and gave himself for me'
(Galatians 2:20). Writing to another group of Christians he
said, 'I consider everything a loss compared to the surpassing
greatness of knowing Christ Jesus my Lord' (Philippians 3:8).

You can now see how plainly the Word of God shows who
are the 'wicked' and who are the 'converted'. Some people
think that if a man is not a drunkard, a fornicator, an extortioner, or such like, and that if he goes to church, or says his
prayers, then he is a converted man. Others think that if
someone who used to be a drunkard or a gambler or had some
other vice has now given this up, then he is a converted man.
Others think that if a person who used to be anti-religious in his
attitudes changes his mind and becomes religious, then he
must surely be converted. Some are even foolish enough to

think that they are converted because they have taken up with some new religious idea or other. And some think that a guilty conscience, a fear of hell, a determination to do better, or an outwardly acceptable civil and religious life is the same as true conversion. Yet all of these are wrong, and in the greatest danger, because when they hear that the wicked must turn or die they think that the warning does not apply to them, either because they are not 'wicked', or because they are already 'converted'. This is why Jesus told some good-living religious leaders of his day that 'The tax collectors and the prostitutes are entering the kingdom of God ahead of you' (Matthew 21:31). He did not mean that tax collectors (who were notorious for their dishonesty) and prostitutes could be saved without conversion, but that it was easier to make gross sinners admit their sin and their need of conversion than those whose sins were more 'respectable' and who deluded themselves by thinking that they were already converted when they were not.

Conversion and its consequences

Conversion is very different from what most people think. It is no small thing to unhinge a person's mind from earth and focus it on heaven, and for a man to have such an appreciation of God that he turns to him with a love that cannot be quenched. It is no small thing to break a man's heart from sin and make him turn to Christ for refuge and thankfully embrace him as the life of his soul; nor to have the very drift and bent of the heart and life changed so that he turns his back on the things in which he thought he found happiness, places his hope for happiness where he never did before and has a totally new direction to his life. The Bible says that the person who is truly converted to Christ is 'a new creation; old things have passed

away; behold, all things have become new' (2 Corinthians
5:17, NKJV). He has a new understanding, a new will, a new
resolution, new sorrows and desires, a new love, new
thoughts, new speech and new companions. Things which
used to be laughing matters to him are now so vile that he runs
from them as if from death. The world that was so lovely in his
eyes now seems to be empty and aggravating. God, once
neglected, is now the happiness of his soul; before, God was
forgotten and every desire preferred before him, but now he
comes before everything else. Jesus Christ, of whom he once
thought so little, is now his only hope and refuge. He depends
on him as on his daily food; he cannot live without him, pray
without him, rejoice without him, think without him or speak
without him. Heaven, which he once thought of in such vague
terms, he now sees as his home, the place of his only hope and
rest, where he will spend all eternity seeing and loving and
praising God. Hell, which he once thought was only an
invention to frighten men from sin, he now sees to be real and
terrible and not something to be risked or toyed with. Holiness
of life, which he once thought to be boring and unnecessary,
is now his one great aim. The Bible, once thought to be no
different from any other book, he now sees as the law of God,
written directly to him and signed with God's own name. It
rules his thoughts, words and deeds. Its commands are bind-
ing, its warnings serious and its promises full of life. God's
people, who once seemed just like other people, are now seen
to be the finest and happiest people in the world, and the
wicked, his careless playfellows, now fill him with sorrow.
Once he laughed at their sin; now he weeps for them and at the
terrible misery their sins will bring to them. He weeps over
those of whom the Bible says, 'Their destiny is destruction;
their god is their stomach and their glory is in their shame.
Their mind is on earthly things' (Philippians 3:19). He now

realizes that all unconverted people are 'enemies of the cross of Christ' (Philippians 3:18).

All of this means that the converted man has a new heart, new thoughts and a new life. Before, self-satisfaction was his only goal in life; now he is taken up with God and his Word. His life is marked by holiness, righteousness and mercy. Before, self ruled his life; everything else, even the voices of God and his own conscience, had to give way; now God rules his life and everything has to give way to him. Conversion is not a change in a few areas of a person's life; it is a revolution in which everything is changed. A man walking in the country can take one of several paths and still be heading in the same general direction; but it is another matter altogether to turn around and walk towards a different destination. So it is with conversion; a man can turn from drunkenness, immorality or some other gross sin and start going to church, yet still be on his self-centred way to hell. But when a person is truly converted, self is dethroned and God is enthroned. Instead of being addicted to self, the converted man is devoted to God. His whole life is pointed in a new direction. Before, he used his time, talents and possessions to gratify his own selfish ends; now he asks for God's direction in all of these areas and seeks to use his gifts to God's glory. Before, he would only do something for God if it was not inconvenient or uncomfortable; now he is determined to please God whatever it costs. This is real conversion, the mighty change that God works in all who are truly saved — and it is a change which every man and woman in the world must experience or they will be condemned to eternal misery.

Has it happened?

Do you believe this? How can you not believe something that is beyond doubt or denial? This is not something about which there is any disagreement among genuine Christians. All of them are agreed on it as being the true teaching of the Word of God, and if you dare to disbelieve what God has clearly spoken you are in serious trouble and without excuse. If you do believe it, why are you content to remain unconverted? Let me put the issue to you in another way. Do you know that you *are* converted? Has this wonderful change taken place in your life? Have you been 'born again' (John 3:3) — given a new life? You may not be able to name the date on which this happened, or the exact words God used to bring it about, but do you know that the work has been done, that the change has taken place, and that your heart is now the kind of heart I have been describing?

Most people care nothing for these things. As long as they are able to say something like, 'I am not a thief, a drunkard, an extortioner,' or 'I go to church,' or 'I say my prayers,' they imagine they are converted. But they are deceiving themselves; they are paying too little attention to the glories of heaven and to their own immortal souls. Are you doing this, making light of heaven and hell? Very soon your body will lie in the dust and your soul will be carried to its eternal destination. Things will soon be very different for you then from what they are at the present! You will live in your present home just a little longer, work just a little longer, see with your eyes, hear with your ears and speak with your tongue just a little longer; then you will die and one day be raised to face God in judgement. Can you dare to ignore this? What a place you will soon be in — one of joy or of torment! What a sight you will soon see — in heaven or hell! What thoughts will overwhelm you — with indescribable delight or horror! What work you will be engaged in — praising God with saints and angels, or crying out with devils in the agony of unquenchable fire! Can you possibly ignore this? And remember that these things will be *endless*; your joys or sorrows will be *eternal*. Can you brush this aside?

When you have travelled a little longer on this earth you will be dead and gone, and then you will find that everything I am telling you is true. Then you will remember reading these pages and being told about these things, and you will realize that they are a thousand times more important than you and I could ever imagine here on earth. How then can you possibly turn them aside? If God had not enabled me to believe these things and take them to heart, I would have remained in selfish, spiritual darkness and perished for ever. But because he has revealed them to me I long to have compassion on others, including you! Surely you can understand this? If you grasped the reality of hell and saw your unconverted neighbours dragged there in terror, even though you thought they were decent people who were unaware of their danger, surely you would want to warn everyone of the terrible danger they were in? Jesus told a parable along similar lines about a man who found himself in hell and cried out that someone should be sent to his five brothers, 'so that they will not also come to this place of torment' (Luke 16:28).

Believing is seeing

But faith is a kind of sight; it is the eye of the soul, the evidence of things we cannot see. If I believe God it is next to seeing him. This is why I am so certain and earnest about these tremendous truths. If a friend of yours died tomorrow and later returned to the earth to tell you what he had seen, would you not be willing to hear him? Would you not believe him and pay attention to what he told you? Would you not want him to speak the truth? And would you not rush to hear him and take to heart whatever

he said? But this will not happen. God's way of teaching you
is through the faithful preaching and teaching of the Scriptures, and he will not change his methods to suit the wishes of
unbelievers. This is why I beg of you to listen to me now as you
would listen to someone who had come back from the dead to
speak to you, because I can assure you of the truth of what I am
saying as fully as if I had seen these things with my own eyes.
After all, it would be possible for someone to come back from
the dead and lie about what he had seen — but Jesus Christ can
never lie, and the Word of God, given to us by the Holy Spirit,
can never deceive you. You must therefore believe these truths
or be lost. If you believe that God's Word is true, if you care
anything for the salvation of your soul, I beg of you to search
your heart and ask yourself these questions: 'Is it really true
that I must turn or die? Must I be converted or condemned?
Surely I should do something about it before it is too late? Why
have I not already done so? Why have I taken a chance and
neglected something so important?' As you turn these questions over in your mind, thank God that he has not already cut
off your earthly life before you had any hope of eternal life.
Then make sure that you do not neglect the matter any longer.
Be honest before God and continue to ask yourself the kind of
questions that will help you to discover whether or not you are
truly converted: 'Has God ever brought about a great change
in my life? Has the Holy Spirit shown me the vileness of sin,
my need of a Saviour, Christ's great love for sinners and the
glories of God and of heaven? Is my heart broken and humbled
when I think of the life I have lived? Have I gladly received
Jesus Christ as my Saviour and Lord? Do I hate my former
sinful life and every remnant of sin there is in me? Do I turn
away from sins as my deadly enemies? Am I determined to live
a life of holiness and obedience to God? Do I love holiness and
delight in obedience? Can I truly say that I am dead to the

world and carnal self and that I live for God and the glory he
has promised? Do I think more of heaven than I do of earth?
Is God more dear to me than anyone else? Instead of my giving
him the left-overs of my life and service, does my life now
have a new direction, a new aim? Have I set my hopes and my
heart on heaven? Am I longing to go there, to see God face to
face and to live for ever in his love and praise? When I sin, is
it against the general inclination of my heart? Is God enabling
me to conquer all gross sins, and do I long to get rid of all moral
weakness?'

This is a searching examination, but it will surely help you
to see whether or not you are truly converted. If you are in any
doubt about where you stand it is time to get your doubt
resolved, because the day is soon coming when the Judge of all
men will resolve it for you. Surely you know yourself well
enough to determine whether or not you are converted? If you
are not, it is no good flattering yourself with pride and false
hopes. Why deceive yourself any longer? Instead, cry out to
God for the grace that will enable you to be converted. If you
delay any longer you run the risk of being forsaken by God or
snatched away by death — and then it will be too late. There
is no place for repentance after death. It must be now or never.

Search your heart!

All I ask of you is this — examine your heart to see whether
or not you are truly converted. If you are still uncertain, try to
find a godly minister of the gospel and ask for his help. The
matter is so important that you should let nothing hinder you
from doing this. Godly ministers are part of God's provision
for the good of our souls, just as doctors are for the good of our
bodies. Thousands of people think they are converted when

they are not. They refuse to listen when we call them to turn to God because they think that as long as they avoid some of the foulest sins they are already converted and moving in the right direction — whereas they are obviously living for themselves and are strangers to God and eternal life. They refuse to think seriously about it and to spend a few hours examining their spiritual condition. If only they knew the danger they were in! If only they knew that a merciful God was prepared to do so much to save them while they themselves do so little! Is this true of you? If so, the devil has blinded your mind and made you believe that you are already saved. If you *knew* that you were not on your way to heaven and would be lost for ever if you died in your present state, would you dare spend another night in sleep? Would you dare live another day in that condition? Would you ever laugh or be happy again, knowing that at any moment you could find yourself snatched away to hell? Surely you would cry to God for a new heart and seek the help of those able to counsel you?

You cannot possibly *want* to be condemned. Then I beg of you to search your heart and go on doing so until you know where you stand. If you find that you are truly converted, then you can rejoice and seek to continue living a life of godliness; if you find you are not, you must give the matter your urgent attention. Will you do this now? Will you examine yourself? Is this an unreasonable request? Your conscience knows it is not. Then do what God commands you, remembering that you must soon appear before him at the Day of Judgement. For the sake of your eternal soul, which must turn or die, make sure that you are standing on firm ground. You dare not risk your soul by being careless or negligent.

3.
God's great promise

The second great principle to be considered is this: *God promises that if the wicked will turn they will receive eternal life.*

As surely as God promises hell to the wicked, so he promises heaven to the converted. 'Turn and live' is as certain a truth as 'Turn or die', and God delights in seeing sinners turn and live. When man sinned and broke off his relationship with God, God was not bound to provide him with a Saviour, nor give him any hope of salvation, nor even to call him to turn to him — yet in his great mercy he has done all of these things. This is the message that all true preachers of the gospel bring to men. Ours is not a message of condemnation; it is exactly the opposite. Our message is that everyone who is born again will be saved. Ours is not a message of despair; it is a message of hope. Life, not death, is what we are proclaiming. Our commission from God is to offer salvation, certain salvation, immediate, glorious and everlasting salvation to everyone —

even to the worst of sinners. God commands us to offer full and free forgiveness to all who will turn to him and live. We are commanded to tell men what Christ has done for sinners, what mercy, patience and kindness God has towards them and what wonderful happiness will be theirs if they will turn to him — and then to urge them to accept God's offer.

Sad and glad

Of course, our message *does* speak of God's anger and of the sinner's death, but this is not our principal message. True preachers of God's Word must certainly warn men that by nature they are already under God's righteous anger and are spiritually dead, but this is to show them their need of God's mercy and to make them realize the value of God's grace. Just as nobody will go to a doctor unless he is convinced that he is ill, so my reason for telling you of the terrible condition you have brought upon yourself is so that you will turn to Christ for mercy. This is also why I am telling you about the eternal torment that will fall on those who refuse to be converted.

But this is the sad part of my message. Firstly, I am to offer you mercy if you will turn to God; it is only those who refuse to turn and who refuse God's voice of mercy to whom I must bring a message of eternal damnation. If you will turn from your sin, turn to Christ and be converted, I have not a damning word to say against you. In the name of the Lord of life I am able to assure you that, however wicked a sinner you are, you will have mercy and salvation if you will turn to Christ. Christ has done everything necessary and God's promise is free, full and eternal. You may have life if you will only turn — but remember what the Scripture means by 'turning'. It is not like repairing an old house; instead, it is like pulling the old one down and building a new one on Jesus Christ, the only sure foundation. It is not a matter of making a few moral changes in your life, but of putting your sinful nature to death and living a life of obedience to the Holy Spirit. It is not a matter of respectability and religion; it means changing your master and the whole aim and purpose of your life. It means setting your face in exactly the opposite direction to the one in which you have been going, and dedicating yourself and all that you have to God. This is the change that must be made if you are to receive eternal life.

This shows you that salvation, not condemnation, is the most important part of my message to you. If you will accept this and turn to Christ, there is no need to trouble or frighten you with talk of damnation. But if you refuse to be saved you will certainly be damned, for there is no middle road; you must have either life or death.

The truth of the matter

But God calls me not only to offer you life, but to show you that God means what he says, that his promise is true and that heaven is not a myth but a real place of true and eternal happiness. There are a hundred places in Scripture where the truth of God's offer can be seen. Here are just some of them.

The Bible says that if anyone becomes a Christian, 'he is a new creation; old things have passed away; behold, all things have become new' (2 Corinthians 5:17, NKJV). When Jesus commissioned the apostles he said, 'Go into all the world and preach the good news to all creation. Whoever believes and is baptized will be saved, but whoever does not believe will be condemned' (Mark 16:15-16). The apostle Paul was able to tell his hearers that 'Through Jesus the forgiveness of sins is proclaimed to you' (Acts 13:38).

You will see from these statements that preachers of the gospel have divine authority to promise you that if you will turn to God you will live. You may safely trust your soul here: 'For God so loved the world that he gave his one and only Son, that whoever believes in him shall not perish but have eternal life' (John 3:16). The blood of the Son of God has purchased the promise; the faithfulness and truth of God guarantee that it is valid; Scripture records many miracles God performed to confirm it; preachers are sent throughout the world to proclaim it; and the Holy Spirit opens men's hearts to receive it. These things are beyond argument. Even the worst of sinners will be saved if he will truly turn to God.

If you think you will be saved without conversion you believe a lie, and I would be telling you a lie if I were to say that you will. It would be like believing what the devil says rather than what God says. After all, both God and the devil promise men eternal life. God's promise is 'Turn and live'; the devil's promise is 'You will live whether you turn or not.' God says, 'Unless you are converted and become as little children, you will by no means enter the kingdom of heaven' (Matthew 18:3, NKJV); 'No one can see the kingdom of God unless he is born again' (John 3:3); 'Without holiness no one will see the Lord' (Hebrews 12:14). On the other hand, the devil says, 'You can be saved without being born again, without being converted. There is no need to be holy; it is enough to be respectable. God is trying to frighten you. He is too merciful to condemn anyone; he will be better to you than his word.' And the tragedy is that most people believe the devil rather than God — which is exactly how sin first came into the world. God told our first parents, 'You must not eat fruit from the tree that is in the middle of the garden, and you must not touch it, or you will die' (Genesis 3:3). But the devil contradicted him and said, 'You will not surely die' (Genesis 3:4); and Adam and Eve believed the devil rather than God. So now God says, 'Turn or die', but the devil says, 'You will not die. Keep on sinning as long as you can, then at the last minute ask God to have mercy on you' — and this is what the world believes. There can be no greater wickedness than to believe the devil rather than God!

Those who believe that they can be saved without a radical change of heart and life may even say they are trusting God, but the fact is that they are doing exactly the opposite — they are believing the devil. They have virtually turned God into Satan. Where did God say that an unregenerate, unconverted, unholy person will be saved? Show me even one place in Scripture where he says this. This is the devil's lie and to believe it is to believe the devil. The Word of God is full of comfort and strength for the person who is holy, but has nothing to support wickedness or give anyone the slightest hope of being saved without a change of heart leading to holiness of life.

However, if you will turn to God's mercy, God's mercy will welcome you. Then trust God for salvation, because he has promised in his Word to save all who do. He will not save any who refuse to forsake the world, the flesh and the devil, but he will be a Father to all who come into his family by trusting his Son. If men will not come in it is their own fault. The door of salvation is wide open. God holds back nobody from entering. He never says to anyone, 'Even if you are converted I will not receive you.' He could have done so and still remained righteous, but he never has and he never will. If you are sincerely ready to turn to him with all your heart, God is ready to receive you and to grant you the forgiveness of sins and eternal life. The truth of this wonderful promise will become even clearer in the next three chapters.

4.
God's good pleasure

This brings us to the third great principle contained in God's message to Ezekiel: *God takes pleasure in men's conversion and salvation, not in their death or damnation; he had rather they would return to him and live than go on in their wickedness and die.*

The Bible says, 'The Lord is not slow in keeping his promise, as some understand slowness. He is patient with you, not wanting anyone to perish, but everyone to come to repentance' (2 Peter 3:9). This shows that God sincerely desires the conversion of all men, even those who will never be converted — yet not in the sense that this is something he has determined to do, or as something he has determined will come to pass. Let me explain. A king may have power to imprison a murderer, and even to execute him, though at the same time his real desire is that his people should not commit murder. He takes no pleasure in executing one of his subjects; he would rather the person concerned had kept the law and lived. In other words,

his subjects' obedience is his desire but not his determination.
Let me put it another way. A king may make a public
proclamation that says, 'I take no pleasure in your death but
rather that you would obey my law and live; but if you commit
a capital offence I have determined that you will die.' In the
same way, a judge could truthfully say to a convicted murderer, 'I take no pleasure in sentencing you to death; I had
rather you had kept the law and lived, but as you have broken
the law I must condemn you or I should be unjust.' The same
principle applies in the issue we are considering. Although
God takes no pleasure in condemning you, and therefore calls
you to turn and live, he does take pleasure in the demonstration
of his own justice and in the execution of his own laws, and has
therefore determined that if you will not be converted you will
be condemned. If God was so much against the condemnation
of the wicked that he determined to do everything he could to
prevent it, then nobody would be condemned. But this is not
the case. Jesus said that 'Small is the gate and narrow the road
that leads to life, and only a few find it' (Matthew 7:14). Yet
God is opposed to your condemnation to this extent: he teaches
you, warns you, invites you to choose between life and death,
and commands preachers of the gospel to urge you not to
destroy yourself but to accept his mercy. But if this is not
enough, and you remain unconverted, then you are without
excuse and God is determined that you will be damned. He
says, 'O wicked man, you will surely die' (Ezekiel 33:8). Jesus
said, 'Assuredly, I say to you, unless you are converted and
become as little children, you will by no means enter the
kingdom of heaven' (Matthew 18:3, NKJV) and 'I tell you the
truth, no one can see the kingdom of God unless he is born
again' (John 3:3). Notice the words 'by no means enter' and
'cannot see' in those last two statements. It is useless to think
otherwise, and to imagine that somehow God will save the
unconverted, because that is something that can never happen.

Proof of the principle

This then is the position. God, the great law-giver of the world, takes no pleasure in the death of the wicked, but would rather that they would turn and live, yet he is determined that none shall live except those who turn. And as a righteous Judge he delights in justice, and in demonstrating his hatred of sin, even though the misery which sinners have brought upon themselves does not in itself give him pleasure. All of this can be proved in five ways.

Firstly, the Bible makes it clear that God is wonderfully gracious. It speaks of 'the Lord, the Lord, the compassionate and gracious God, slow to anger, abounding in love and faithfulness, maintaining love to thousands, and forgiving wickedness, rebellion and sin' (Exodus 34:6-7). The same kind of thing is said in many other places in the Bible and should assure you that God takes no pleasure in your condemnation.

Secondly, if God took more pleasure in your condemnation than in your conversion he would not have so often commanded you in his Word to turn, or given you so many reasons to persuade you, or made you such promises of eternal life if you do turn.

Thirdly, if God took more pleasure in your condemnation than your conversion and salvation he would never have commissioned ministers of the gospel to remind you of your sins, warn you of your danger, offer you God's mercy and teach you the way of life — and to continue doing so, even when they are hated and abused by the very people they are trying to help. Would God have gone to all of this trouble if his principal pleasure was in your condemnation?

Fourthly, it is proved by God's gracious providence. If God had rather you were damned than converted and saved he

would not have reinforced his Word with his works. He would
not have given you all the daily mercies of life which are meant
to turn your heart towards him. The Bible specifically asks,
'Do you show contempt for the riches of his kindness, tolerance and patience, not realizing that God's kindness leads you
towards repentance?' (Romans 2:4). He would not have tried
to bring you to your senses by punishing you at times. He
would not have waited so patiently for you day after day and
year after year. These are not the actions of someone who takes
pleasure in your death. If that had been the case, God could
easily have had you in hell a long time ago. How many times
could he have snatched you away in the midst of your sins?
When you were lying, or proud, or dishonest, or deriding
God's ways, how easily he could have stopped your breath and
brought you to your senses in eternity! What an easy thing it
is for the Almighty God to tie the hands of the most malicious
persecutor, end the fury of the bitterest of his enemies and let
them know that they are but worms! God only has to frown
upon you and you would drop into your grave. If he commanded his angels to go out and destroy ten thousand sinners,
it would be done in a moment. How easily God could strike
you down with pain and sickness and make you eat the words
you have spoken against his Word, his worship and his works,
so that you would cry out for the prayers of those you once
despised! How easily he could make your body too weak to
hold your soul! How quickly he could reduce to nothing that
body of yours, which must have everything it wants — even
if it means disobeying God! When you were at your worst,
defending your sin and arguing with those who pleaded with
you to leave it, how easily could God have snatched you into
eternity to face him in judgement, and then asked you, 'Now
what do you say against your Creator, his truth, his servants or
his holy ways? What is the best case you can make for

yourself? What excuse can you give for your sins? Give an account of your sins, the use of your time and your abuse of my mercies.' If God had done this, your stubborn heart would have melted, your pride been shattered, and your boasting words turned to speechless silence or fearful cries. And how easily God could do this now, at any time! One word from his mouth and all your present powers would be lost.

But God has done none of this; instead, he has patiently and mercifully upheld you. Day after day he has given you the very breath you use to live a godless life. He has given you mercies which you have used to gratify your own sinful desires. He has given you provisions which you have used to satisfy your own greed. He has given you every minute of time that you have wasted in idleness or worldliness. Does all of this patience, mercy and provision not show you that God takes no pleasure in your damnation? Can the candle burn without wax? Can your house stand without the earth holding it up? Nor can you live a single hour without God's support. And why has he supported your life for so long but to see when you would come to your senses, turn to him and receive eternal life? Would anyone arm his enemies, or hold a light for a murderer who was killing his children, or help an employee to play or sleep when he should be working? Surely the reason that God has been so patient with you is to give you an opportunity to turn to him and live.

Fifthly, the suffering and death of his Son, Jesus Christ, proves that God takes no pleasure in the death of the wicked. Would God have come to earth and taken our humanity into the Godhead? Would the Lord Jesus Christ have lived a life of suffering and then died in the place of sinners, bearing the judgement for their sin, if he had preferred their condemnation? We are told that he 'healed many who had various diseases' (Mark 1:34); that 'he spent the night praying to God' (Luke 6:12); that on at least one occasion he prayed so earnestly that 'his sweat was like drops of blood falling to the ground' (Luke 22:44); and after a lifetime of service he allowed himself to be put to death in the place of others, bearing the punishment which they deserved.

Are these the actions of one who delights in the death of the wicked? He did all this for sinners. His sacrifice is sufficient for all sinners — and you are a sinner. Yet it was never his intention to save any who would not turn to him in repentance and faith. Time and again he expressed his sorrow at men's disobedience and impatience. When he went to Jerusalem for the last time he wept over the city and cried, 'O Jerusalem, Jerusalem, you who kill the prophets and stone those sent to you, how often I have longed to gather your children together, as a hen gathers her chicks under her wings, but you were not willing' (Matthew 23:37). Even when dying on the cross he prayed for his persecutors, 'Father, forgive them, for they do not know what they are doing' (Luke 23:34). Are those the words of someone whose greatest desire is the death of the wicked, even those who perish because of their wilful unbelief? When we read, 'For God so loved the world that he gave his one and only Son, that whoever believes in him shall not perish but have eternal life' (John 3:16), we have all the evidence we need that God takes no pleasure in the death of the wicked but that he longs for them to turn to him and live.

5.
God's word of honour

The mere word of God ought to be sufficient to convince men of its truth, but such is the depravity of the human heart that they are prepared to argue with what God has said, even on issues that concern their eternal destiny. It is at this point that we come across the fourth great principle contained in God's message to Ezekiel: *God is so concerned that men should not question these truths that he solemnly confirms them with an oath.*

If you dare question God's word I hope you will not dare question his oath. Just as Jesus solemnly said that 'Unless you are converted and become as little children, you will by no means enter the kingdom of heaven' (Matthew 18:3, NKJV) and 'I tell you the truth, no one can see the kingdom of God unless he is born again' (John 3:3), so God has not only *said* that his pleasure is not in the death of the wicked but in their life; he has *sworn* it. The Bible puts it like this: 'When God made his promise to Abraham, since there was no one greater for him to swear by, he swore by himself, saying, "I will surely bless you and give you many descendants." And so after waiting patiently, Abraham received what was promised. Men swear by someone greater than themselves, and the oath confirms what is said and puts an end to all argument. Because God wanted to make the unchanging nature of his purpose very clear to the heirs of what was promised, he confirmed it with an oath. God did this so that, by two unchangeable things in which it is impossible for God to lie, we who have fled to take hold of the hope offered to us may be greatly encouraged' (Hebrews 6:13-18). This should put an end to all of man's arguments about things like predestination or whether God does actually condemn the wicked. These arguments merely serve to show man's ignorance, whereas the fact is that God confirms his intentions by an oath which leaves nothing in doubt.

Who wants you to be lost?

If you are an unconverted sinner I beg of you to think carefully on these things and ask yourself this: 'Who is it that takes pleasure in my sin and damnation?' It is certainly not God. He says — and swears — that he takes no pleasure in it. And in any case you are certainly not trying to please God. You dare not say that you lie, steal, or cheat, or are proud or immoral, or neglect church-going, Bible-reading and prayer in order to please God; that would be like trying to overthrow a king and saying that you were doing it for his pleasure.

Then who takes pleasure in your sin and damnation? It is certainly not those who are Christians. It gives no pleasure to faithful ministers of the gospel or to any Christian friends you may have to see you serving the devil and running headlong into hell. It gives them no pleasure to see such blindness, carelessness, stubborness and presumption, or to see you so determined to continue in your sinful ways and to resist their appeal to you to change. They know that you are under God's righteous judgement and that this will end in everlasting disaster for you. They get no more pleasure from it than a doctor does in realizing that a patient has contracted a terminal disease. It saddens them that you are heading for hell and that they seem unable to stop you. It hurts them to know how easily you could escape if you were willing. Those of us who are Christians would do anything we could to save you. Those who are preachers of the gospel study day and night to know what to say to convince and persuade you. We show you chapter and verse from God's Word, which makes it crystal clear that you cannot be saved unless you are converted, hoping that if you will not believe us, you will at least believe what God says — and still you refuse to do anything about it.

A preacher's prayer

But we do something else that you know nothing about — we agonize in prayer for you. At times we tell God, 'We have spoken to them in your name, we have told them what you told us to tell them, we have warned them of the dangers of being unconverted, we have repeated your very words — "There is no peace for the wicked"' (Isaiah 57:21) — but even the worst of them will not so much as admit that they are wicked. We have reminded them that "If you live according to the sinful nature, you will die" (Romans 8:13). They pretend to believe in you, but go on living in a way that shows they are prepared to ignore your warnings and to hope that you will not condemn anyone. They refuse to believe that "When a wicked man dies, his hope perishes; all he expected from his power comes to nothing" (Proverbs 11:7).

'We tell them what a vile, worthless thing sin is, but they love it and refuse to leave it. We warn them they will pay for their sin in everlasting punishment and death, but they refuse to believe it and are prepared to take a chance on your mercy. We tell them how willing you are to receive them — and it only makes them put off turning to you even longer. We plead with them, urge them, offer them our help, but we can do nothing with them. The drunkards remain drunkards, the ignorant ignorant, the proud proud, the immoral immoral and the selfish selfish. Few are prepared to acknowledge their sin, and even fewer to forsake it; they seem happy to settle for the fact that all men are sinners, as if there was no difference between a converted sinner and one who remains unconverted.

'Some will not even listen to us; they think they already know all they need to know; some listen, but then ignore everything we say and go on doing what they like; some have no more feeling than a corpse — when we talk to them about things that will affect them for eternity, not a word seems to touch them.

'When we refuse to join them in their sinful ways they hate us and criticize us, and if we urge them to confess and forsake their sins in order to save themselves they refuse point blank. They want us to disobey God and damn our souls to please them, but they will not turn and save their souls to please God. They think they are wiser than their teachers, and nothing we do seems to shift them from their ways. Lord, we are helpless; we see these people ready to drop into hell, and we are unable to stop them. We know that if they would sincerely turn from their sins they would be saved, and we cannot persuade them, not even if we get on our knees in tears and beg them to do so. What more can we do?'

That is how true gospel preachers feel and pray. Did you ever realize that? And do you think they take any delight in seeing sinners continue in their sin, cheerfully hurrying to hell? Do you think they enjoy being unable to stop you, even though they know the everlasting suffering that awaits you and what everlasting joy you are deliberately throwing away? There is nothing you could do that could hurt them more! It grieves them deeply to see you in such a state. It breaks their hearts, even if it is of little or no concern to you.

Satan and self

Of course there is someone who takes pleasure in your sin — and that is the devil. After all, the whole purpose of his temptations is to lead you into sin and drag you down to destruction. Nothing would please him better than for you to go on sinning. He loves it when you are proud, impure or greedy, when you lie, steal, swear or commit some other sin. But it is not only the devil who is happy to see you sinning. The wicked are equally happy, because it makes them feel comfortable in their own sinful ways.

Yet you are not sinning to please the devil or other sinners; instead, the reason you sin is to please your own sinful nature. This is your most dangerous enemy! It is your sinful nature that demands to be pampered and that insists on having its demands met, in the food you eat, the clothes you wear, the company you keep — in everything that you think, say or do. It is your sinful nature that is always demanding attention, always insisting on being satisfied. This is the god you are serving, and it will swallow up everything you give it.

Let me ask you some questions about this. Firstly, is it right to serve your sinful nature rather than your Creator? Are you happy to displease God, all faithful preachers of the gospel and any Christian friends you may have in order to satisfy your own selfish desires? Is God not worthy to be your master? Then remember, if God does not rule you he will not save you.

Secondly, your sinful nature may be pleased with your sin, but is your conscience pleased? Does it not sometimes remind you that things are not what they should be and that one day there will be a price to pay? And is it not more important to quieten your conscience than to satisfy your sinful nature?

Thirdly, have you never realized that your sinful nature is digging its own grave? It loves all the 'good things' — food, drink, leisure, fun, wealth, popularity, pride of position and possessions — but does it love what happens at the end of a godless life? Does it love the idea of standing before God on the Day of Judgement and being condemned to everlasting fire? Does it relish being tormented with the devils for ever? Remember, sin and hell can only be separated by true conversion. If you like the idea of eternal punishment in hell, no wonder you want to go on sinning. But if not (and I am sure that this is the case) is any sin worth the loss of eternal life? Is a little pleasure, or leisure or self-satisfaction worth losing heaven for? Are temporary, earthly possessions worth more than eternal, heavenly riches? Are they worth the sufferings of eternal fire? Think about these things before you go any further.

Let me say it again: God swears that he has no pleasure in your death and condemnation, but rather that you would turn and live. Yet if you would rather die than turn, remember that you are doing so not to please God but to please yourself. If you will condemn yourself in order to please yourself, if you will take pleasure in running headlong into hell and refuse to respond to a God who longs to rescue you, then you must take the consequences; you will come to your senses one day, but by then it will be too late.

6.
God's continuous concern

The fact that God swears that he takes no pleasure in the condemnation of the wicked is a powerful indication of its truth, but he goes even further in this fifth principle: *God is so zealous for the conversion of sinners that he repeats and emphasizes his commands and persuasions to them to turn to him and live.*

In the light of what we have already seen, who can possibly doubt that God's great desire is that the wicked should turn to him and live? In this chapter I want you to see something of the earnestness with which God longs for this. This is obvious by the way in which he repeats his exhortation: *'Turn! Turn from your evil ways!'* How can you refuse to listen to Almighty God when he speaks like that? If God told you that you were to die tomorrow you would not treat it lightly — yet here is something equally serious because it concerns your

eternal destiny. It is both a command and an exhortation. It is
as if God were saying, 'As your Creator, I *command* you to
renounce the world, the flesh and the devil and to turn to me;
yet as One who is lovingly concerned about your eternal
welfare I *plead* with you to turn so that you will escape the
fearful result of your sin.' How can anyone refuse such a
message, such a command and such a plea as this?

Here, beyond all question, is the most joyful message that
anyone has ever heard: 'Turn! Turn ...Why will you die? You
are not yet finally condemned; you can still escape going to
hell. Here is God's offer of mercy, pardon, forgiveness and
eternal life. Turn to him and all of these things will be yours.'
Surely you should be overwhelmed with joy to hear such
news? You may have heard the gospel before, but how have
you responded to it? And how do you respond to it now? To
every careless, ignorant sinner in the world, God says, 'Turn
... and you will live.' To every glutton, every drunkard, every
liar in the world, God says, 'Turn ... and you will live.' To the
one who claims falsely to be a Christian but knows nothing of
the power of Christ's cross and resurrection, God says, 'Turn
... and you will live.' To all who know nothing of God's love,
whose hearts are not taken up with him, who are more
concerned about earth than they are with heaven, who try to
get by with a little religion, who have not been willing to
forsake anything and everything for Christ, God says, 'Turn
... and you will live.' If you have never heard these things until
reading this book, remember that you have heard them now!
If you turn to God through faith in Christ you will receive
eternal life; if you do not turn you will be condemned for ever.

What will you do? Will you turn or will you not? 'How
long will you waver between two opinions?' (1 Kings 18:21).
If God is God, then turn to him and serve him; if your sinful
nature is your god, then carry on as you are. If heaven is better

than earth, then turn in that direction and begin to 'store up for yourselves treasures in heaven, where moth and rust do not destroy, and where thieves do not break in and steal' (Matthew 6:20). Seek to enter that kingdom 'that cannot be shaken' (Hebrews 12:28) and begin to live on a higher plane. But if you think that earth is better than heaven, or will do more for you, or will last you longer, then keep it and make the best of it — but you will be making a fearful and fatal mistake! Let me give you three further reasons to help you make up your mind.

Thinking it through

Firstly, think of all that God in his mercy has done to make salvation available to you — and then think of what a tragedy it is that a man should be damned after all. There was a time (soon after man's first fall into sin) when there was no way back to God. Instead, as the Bible puts it, there was 'a flaming sword flashing back and forth to guard the way to the tree of life' (Genesis 3:24). If things had remained like that there would be nothing that you or anyone else could do to have your sins forgiven and get right with God. But Christ changed all that. He did so by dying on the cross in the place of sinners, bearing in his own body and spirit the penalty which man's sin demanded and deserved. In the Bible's words, 'God was reconciling the world to himself in Christ' (2 Corinthians 5:19). Now he offers forgiveness of sins to all who will accept his offer. Jesus once said that his offer was like an invitation to a banquet, when the host says, 'Come, for everything is now ready' (Luke 14:17). God is ready to welcome you and forgive you for all your sins — if you will come. No matter how wilful and wicked you have been, God will cast all your sins behind his back—if you will come. If you have deliberately run away from God he is ready to meet you, throw his arms around you and rejoice in your conversion — if you will come. God is ready to welcome the vilest of sinners — if they will come. You must have a heart of stone if this does not move you! The eternal and Almighty God, whom you have abused and neglected for so long, and who would be perfectly justified in condemning you for ever, is standing with open arms waiting to welcome you, receive you and forgive you. Is your heart not melted by this? Have you not got more reason to come than God has to invite you?

But that is not all. Christ died on the cross to make a way for you to come to the Father, so that on the basis of his death you would be welcome if you came. Are you still not ready? Every true minister of the gospel is ready to help you, to teach you, to pray for you. Are you still not ready? Every Christian is ready to rejoice at your conversion and welcome you into the fellowship of God's people. As God will forgive you, so they will forgive you as your changed life proves the reality of your conversion. As God will not hold so much as a single sin against you, neither will they. Instead, they are ready to receive you and to welcome you with open arms. Are you still not ready? What is more, heaven itself is ready. God will receive you into everlasting glory with all of his people. However vile you may have been, you may have a place before his throne. Just think of it! God is ready, Christ's sacrifice is ready, the gospel promises are ready, God's free pardon of all your sins is ready, God's people are ready, heaven itself is ready; all are ready and waiting for your conversion. Are you still not ready?

Are you not ready to live when you have been spiritually dead for so long? Are you not ready to come to your senses when you have been out of your mind for so long? Are you not ready to be saved even when you are on the brink of being condemned? Are you not ready to lay hold of Christ, who would save you when you are sinking into damnation? Are you not ready to be rescued from hell when you are ready to be thrown into it? Do you understand what you are doing? If you die unconverted you are sure to be damned — and there is no guarantee that you will live for another hour. Are you still not ready to turn to God? If that is the case, what a miserable wretch you are! Have you not served the devil and self long enough? Have you not yet had enough of sin? Is sin proving to be so profitable to you? Do you know what sin really is, that you want so much more of it? Has God given you so many mercies, so many examples, so many warnings, and spoken to you so many times, and still you are not ready to turn to him? Have you seen so many friends and members of your family laid in their graves, and are still not ready to come to Christ? After so many convictions and pangs of conscience, so many good resolutions, so many promises to do better, are you still not ready to turn to God with all your heart? Oh that God would open your eyes and your heart so that you would understand what an invitation he gives to you to 'come for all things are now ready'!

The voices of God

Secondly, think how many times you have already been called — and remember that the One who calls you is the Sovereign Lord of the universe. God commands the sun to rise, and it does so exactly as he ordains. He commands every planet and star in the heavens to obey him, and they do. He commands the sea to ebb and flow and all of creation to keep its course, and they all obey him. The angels are all 'ministering spirits'

(Hebrews 1:14) fulfilling his every command. Yet when he commands sinful men to turn to him, they refuse to obey him. The sinner thinks he is wiser than God. He argues the case for staying in his sins and he refuses to obey God. Think of it! God only has to speak the word and the very heavens obey him, but when he calls the sinner to deny himself, put his sinful nature to death and set his heart in a new direction, he refuses!

Here is a reliable test as to whether or not you are truly converted: Jesus said, 'I am the good shepherd; I know my sheep and my sheep know me' and they 'listen to my voice' (John 10:14,16). Do you not recognize the voice of God calling you to true repentance and faith? If you do, remember that God is not to be trifled with. Are you determined to go on despising his Word, resisting his Spirit and shutting your ears to his call? Then who do you think will come off worst? Do you realize with whom you are quarrelling, who it is you are disobeying? Do you know what you are doing? It would be easier and wiser for you to walk on thorns with your bare feet, or put your head into a blazing fire! The Bible warns, 'Do not be deceived: God cannot be mocked' (Galatians 6:7). Anyone else can be mocked, but not God. You would be better off playing with fire on the roof of your house than playing with the fire of God's holy anger against sin, because 'Our "God is a consuming fire"' (Hebrews 12:29). The Bible says, 'It is a fearful thing to fall into the hands of the living God' (Hebrews 10:31, NKJV)—and it is therefore just as fearful to argue with him or resist him. God says that a man fighting against him is like briers and thorns fighting against the fire:

'If only there were briers and thorns confronting me!
    I would march against them in battle;
    I would set them all on fire.
Or else let them come to me for refuge;

> let them make peace with me,
> yes let them make peace with me'
>
> .(Isaiah 27:4-5).

Briers and thorns are no match for fire — and the sinner is no match for God.

Have you ever thought how often God has called you to turn, or how many means he has used? Every page of the Bible is like a voice calling out to you, 'Turn or you will die! Turn and live!' Can you read a single page of Scripture and not realize that God is calling you to live? Every evangelistic sermon you may have heard called you to turn; the whole purpose of true gospel preaching is to call and persuade and urge sinners to turn to Christ. The Holy Spirit urges you to turn, and has spoken to you in many ways. Your own conscience has spoken to you. Are you not sometimes convinced that all is not well with you? Does your own conscience not tell you from time to time that you need to change? The lives of godly Christians call you to turn. The quality of their lives rebukes your sin and calls you to turn to God. All of God's works are calling you to turn. They are like books showing you God's greatness, wisdom and mercy. The Bible says,

> 'The heavens declare the glory of God;
> the skies proclaim the work of his hands.
> Day after day they pour forth speech;
> night after night they display knowledge'
>
> (Psalm 19:1-2).

Every time the sun rises it is as if it were saying, 'Why do I circle the world except to show men the glory of their Maker and to give them light so that they can do his will? And do I still find them living in the darkness of sin, sleeping away a life of negligence?

"Wake up, O sleeper,
    rise from the dead,
and Christ will shine on you'"

(Ephesians 5:14).

It was a similar kind of verse from the Bible which led to the conversion of Augustine, one of the most famous Christians in history: 'The night is nearly over; the day is almost here. So let us put aside the deeds of darkness and put on the armour of light. Let us behave decently, as in the daytime, not in orgies and drunkenness, not in sexual immorality and debauchery, not in dissension and jealousy. Rather, clothe yourselves with the Lord Jesus Christ, and do not think about how to gratify the desires of the sinful nature' (Romans 13:12-14). All of God's mercies call you to turn to him. Why does the earth sustain you, but to seek and serve God? Why does it yield food, but to make you serve him? Why does the air allow you to breathe it, but to serve him? Why do other created beings give you the benefit of their labour and their lives, but so that you might serve him? Why does God give you time and health and strength, except to serve him? Why have you food and drink and clothing, but for his service? All of these are God's gracious gifts to you. Surely it is only reasonable for you to consider who gives these to you and why they are given?

God has spared you for year after year and still you have not turned to him. Are you not ashamed? Jesus once told a parable about a man who had a fig tree which bore no fruit for three successive years. He ordered one of his workmen to cut it down, but the workman asked him to give it just one more year, and then if it still had no fruit he would destroy it. The lesson is obvious and serious. For how many years has God been looking for the fruit of holiness in your life — and still there is none? How many times, when you were being deliberately careless and disobedient might you have provoked God to cut you down? Yet in his mercy he has been patient with you and spared you. If you had any understanding at all you would realize that God's patience and mercy were calling you to turn to him: 'Do you think you will escape God's judgement? Or do you show contempt for the riches of his kindness, tolerance and patience, not realizing that God's kindness leads you towards repentance?' (Romans 2:3-4).

And surely every affliction you experience causes you to turn to God? Sickness and pain cry, 'Turn!' Poverty, the death of friends and every other painful experience all cry, 'Turn!' These things have surely made you think! Will they not make you turn? Your own body and being call you to turn to God. Why do you have reason and understanding, except to know God's will and do it? Why do you have a heart, with its ability to love, fear and desire, except to love, fear and desire God best and most of all?

Put all of this together and see what it adds up to. The Bible, the Holy Spirit, gospel preachers, Christian friends, the whole of creation, God's patience, mercies and afflictions and your own human nature, with its powers of reason and emotion — all of them cry, 'Turn to God!' Are you still determined not to do so?

Thirdly, have you never thought seriously about where you stand in relation to the God who calls you to turn to him? You owe him everything you are and everything you have; does he not have the right to command your obedience? You are his servant and should serve no other master. You are at God's mercy and your life is in his hands. You are already under God's wrath because of your sin, and you have no idea how much longer his patience with you will last. This may be the last year, perhaps the last day. His sword is at your heart even while he is speaking to you, and if you do not turn you are dead and undone. If you could see that you were standing on the brink of hell, and how many millions are there already, you would see that it is time to do something about it. How does God's offer affect you? You know now that he longs for you to turn to him and calls you to do so. It is a fearful thing if this does not move you or only half moves you — and it is even more fearful if you shrug off God's offer of mercy and become even more careless.

What good news it would be to those now in hell if they heard such a message from God! And what a welcome word it would seem to you if you had been there for even an hour! Or if you had been there a thousand years — or ten thousand — you would long to hear God inviting you to turn to him. By then it will be too late, yet here and now God offers you the forgiveness of sins and eternal life. It is as if Christ stands in front of you with heaven in one hand and hell in the other and offers you a choice. Then which would you choose? In a voice of infinite love, pity and compassion he says, 'Turn and live,' and asks the question, 'Why will you die?' He knows exactly where you stand and he knows exactly what will happen to you if you refuse to turn. He knows that if you will not turn he will have to deal with you in justice according to his righteous law. That is why he calls you to turn. If you knew a thousandth part of what God knows about the danger you are in and the misery you are heading for, I would not have to write another word to persaude you! What is more, the voice that calls you now is the same one to which millions have already responded. Everyone now in heaven heard that same voice, and not one of them is sorry that they were converted. Not one of them wishes they had neglected God's call. They all know that the voice they heard was the voice of love calling them to eternal salvation — and if you obey the same call you will one day join them in their happiness. There are millions who will regret for ever that they did not turn to God in their lifetime, but there is not a single soul in heaven that regrets having done so.

What more can I say? What will you do? Will you turn or not? Give God your answer. Tell him clearly in case he takes your silence as refusal, and tell him quickly in case he withdraws his offer. Before you move from where you are sitting, determine that by the grace of God you will turn from your sinful ways and surrender your life to him. Do it while you can! You are not yet in hell, nor are you in the terrible position of knowing nothing of the gospel. Eternal life is being offered to you as a free gift if you will only accept it. God offers you the forgiveness of sins and the power of Christ to enable you to live a holy life. If you say nothing, or if you say 'No', then God and your own conscience are witnesses that you have had a fair and generous offer. If you refuse it, remember that you might have had forgiveness of sins, eternal life and the daily enabling of Christ to live for God, but that you forfeited all these because you refused to turn. What possible reasons can you give for this?

7.
God's amazing condescension

The last two chapters have shown that God emphasizes his concern for men's salvation by swearing its truth with an oath and by repeating his invitation to sinners to turn to him and live. These two truths should humble and amaze us, but even they are not as amazing as the sixth principle which I must bring to your attention: *God condescends to reason the case with the wicked; he asks them, 'Why will you die?'*

Here are two factors, both so remarkable that they are almost beyond belief. The first is that men should deliberately be willing to destroy themselves rather than turn to God; the second is that a holy God should be willing to 'discuss' the issue with ungodly, unconverted sinners.

Death-wish

Think of the first of these. Surely it is remarkable that anyone would be willing to die and be damned — let alone that this should be true of most people in the world? Nature teaches us that everyone aims for his own preservation and happiness, and as the wicked are more selfish than others, surely they would be more determined than anyone not to be condemned? That would seem to make sense, but the fact of the matter is that even though the sinner does not want to be condemned eternally, he deliberately chooses to live in a way that guarantees this will happen. God says of the wicked, 'Their deeds are evil deeds ...Their feet rush into sin ...Their thoughts are evil thoughts; ruin and destruction mark their ways. The way of peace they do not know...' (Isaiah 59:6-8), and more than once declares, 'There is no peace for the wicked' (Isaiah 48:22; 57:21). Yet the wicked are determined to ignore everything that God says and go on living as they do. God says that 'Friendship with the world is hatred towards God' (James 4:4) and that if anyone loves the world 'the love of the Father is not in him' (1 John 2:15), yet the wicked are determined to remain wicked, the worldly to remain worldly and the sensual to remain sensual. Although they can hardly relish the idea of spending eternity in hell they are in love with the road that leads to it.

Is this not true of you? You do not want to burn in hell, but you do want to live in the sin which kindles the fire. You do not want to be tormented for ever, but you want to do those things that will bring this about. It is as if you were to say, 'I want to drink this poison, but not to die,' or 'I want to throw myself off the top of a building, but not to kill myself,' or 'I want to stab myself in the heart, but not to take away my life,' or 'I want to set fire to my house, but not to burn it down.' The wicked are just as senseless; they want to live godless lives, but not come to a godless end. But they are ignoring God's law of cause and effect. The person who swallows poison may as well say, 'I want to kill myself,' because that is what will happen. Even if he enjoyed the taste and was not convinced that it was poison, the result would be the same. In the same way, if you are determined to be selfish, immoral, dishonest or worldly, you may as well say, 'I want to be damned,' because you certainly will be unless you turn to God. Would you not condemn the stupidity of anyone who said, 'I want to commit a crime, but I refuse to take the consequences'? Yet the person who says, 'I want to go on living a sinful life,' may as well say, 'I want to go to hell.'

But there is another angle to this, and that is that the wicked deliberately refuse to use the means of salvation which God has provided. The person who refuses to eat may as well say, 'I refuse to live', unless he has found a way of living without food. The person who falls into deep water and refuses to allow anyone to rescue him may as well say, 'I want to drown.' In the same way, if you refuse to listen to what God says, or to use the means of salvation which he has provided, you may as well say, 'I want to be damned,' because if you have found a way to be saved without being converted, you have done something that has never been done before.

But this is not all. The wicked are actually unwilling to experience salvation and all that that means. For instance, although they may have some vague wish to go to heaven when they die, their hearts are in fact opposed to all that heaven means. The Bible teaches that to be in heaven is to be in a state of perfect holiness and of continual love and praise to God, and this has no appeal to the wicked. Even the imperfect worship of God here on earth is something they have little or no time for, much less the endless and perfect worship of heaven. The joys of heaven are so pure and spiritual that the heart of the wicked can never truly desire them. This is why God says that the wicked want to destroy themselves. They refuse to turn, even though they must turn or die. They would rather go on living a life that is bound to end in misery than be converted, and yet they hope that somehow they will eventually spend eternity in some kind of 'heaven'.

The stooping God

But there is a second reason why the whole issue is so remarkable, and that is that God should stoop so low as to plead his case with sinners who are so blind and obstinate about something which is so plain and in which their eternal destiny is at stake. When God sent one of his prophets to preach to the Israelites he warned him of the response he could expect: 'But the house of Israel is not willing to listen to you because they are not willing to listen to me, for the whole house of Israel is hardened and obstinate' (Ezekiel 3:7). Yet when God accuses sinners of despising him, they have the nerve to ask, 'How have we shown contempt for your name?' (Malachi 1:6).

Why is God willing to reason the case out with man? Firstly, because when he created him God gave man powers of reason so that he might use them to God's glory. There is nothing clearer or more reasonable than the offer of salvation. God makes such an offer in terms which man should understand. Secondly, because man should be able to see that God is not asking anything unreasonable. In everything he forbids or commands God has all the reason in the world on his side and man, for his part, has every reason to obey God and none to disobey him. This means that even those who eventually find themselves eternally condemned will be forced to admit that God was right and that they should have turned to him; and they will equally be forced to admit that they were wrong and had no reason to condemn themselves by refusing God's gracious offer of salvation.

Apply this to your own case. What do you say? Are you ready to argue with God? Are you able to prove him wrong? God asks, 'Why will you die?' Have you got an answer to the question? Will you try to prove that God is wrong and you are right? That is quite an undertaking! Certainly one or other of you is in the right and the other in the wrong. God is in favour of your conversion and you are against it. God calls you to turn and you refuse. God calls you to do so today — now; you want to put it off, thinking you have plenty of time. God says that you must be born again and live a holy life; you think that a few little changes here and there will be sufficient. Now who is in the right — God or you? God calls you to turn to him and live a holy life and you refuse to do so because you do not want to. But why not? Can you give any reason that is worth the name?

Although I am only your fellow creature, I dare to challenge you on this, even if I only had these two grounds for doing so, as I am sure that you have no sound reason on your side. No reason can be sound that is against the God of truth and reason. Light can never be opposed to the sun. All knowledge comes from God, so no one can be wiser than God. It would be fatally presumptuous for the highest angel in heaven to claim comparison with his Creator; then how can an ignorant human being, a lump of earth by comparison, set himself against the wisdom of God? It is one of the clearest indications of the vileness and spiritual madness of unconverted men that they dare to contradict their Maker or call in question the Word of God. Men who cannot even understand the basic teachings of Christianity are so conceited in their ignorance that they dare to question the plainest truths of God's Word, contradict them, argue against them, and will accept only those things that agree with their own foolish 'wisdom'!

The absence of reason

It is because I know that God must be in the right that I am sure
no man can bring an argument against him. Can a man have
any reason to break his Maker's laws or dishonour his glory?
Can a man have any reason for damning his own immortal
soul? Remember the question: 'Why will you die?' Is eternal
death something to be cherished? Are you in love with hell?
What reason can you give for deliberately perishing? The
Bible says that 'The wages of sin is death' (Romans 6:23); do
you have any reason to condemn yourself, body and soul, for
ever? What a thing it is for a man to go on sinning against God
and to throw away his everlasting happiness, and yet not to be
able to give any good reason for doing so! If you had a
kingdom offered to you for every sin you cared to commit, it
would not be reason but madness to accept it. If sinning could
bring you the greatest earthly rewards you could ever have,
there would still be no good reason for sinning. If it would
please your greatest friends, or save your own life, or help you
to escape from the greatest earthly misery, it would still make
no sense to commit a single sin. In the same way Jesus said, 'If
your right eye causes you to sin, gouge it out and throw it away.
It is better for you to lose one part of your body than for your
whole body to be thrown into hell' (Matthew 5:29). Eternal
things are so important that nothing on earth can be compared
to them, and not even the greatest of earthly positions can
provide a good enough reason for neglecting an issue that is of
everlasting consequence. No man can give a good reason for
ruining his eternal destiny. Heaven is such a thing that if you
lose it nothing else can take its place, and hell is such a thing
that if you experience it nothing can end your agony. In the
same way, nothing can excuse you for neglecting your own
salvation. As Jesus put it, 'What will it profit a man if he gains

the whole world, and loses his own soul? Or what will a man give in exchange for his soul?' (Mark 8:36, NKJV). If you would only realize the truth of these things, you would soon come to a different opinion about them. If the devil could reach Christians now in heaven and offer them earthly pleasures to draw them away from God and his glory, how do you think they would react? If he offered to make them kings on the earth, do you think that would entice them to leave heaven? Certainly not! They would pour holy scorn on the very idea. And if you could see heaven with the eye of faith you would do the same. Every soul in hell realizes that it was insane to let heaven go for the sake of earthly pleasure, and that no amount of fun or enjoyment or riches or honour can quench hell's fire. If you would only listen to the Word of God you would agree with me that there can be no reasonable warrant for you to destroy your soul; you would not dare to go to bed before you had made up your mind to turn and live.

To save his own life, a man might even cut off an arm or a leg. When Archbishop Thomas Cranmer was being put to death at the stake in 1556 he deliberately thrust his right hand into the fire first to show his repentance at having signed a document which denied what he truly believed. The Bible tells us of those Christian martyrs who 'were tortured and refused to be released' but they had a reason for what they did — it was 'so that they might gain a better resurrection' (Hebrews 11:35). Thousands of others have been prepared to die for their faith, knowing that they would receive their reward in heaven, but for a man to turn his back on his Creator, run headlong into hell when he had been warned about it, and refuse an offer of salvation, is something that no reason in the world can justify or excuse. Heaven will compensate for anything we lose to obtain it, or repay anything we do to gain it. But nothing can ever pay for its loss.

Again, apply this to your own case. As you cannot possibly produce any reason for destroying yourself, what reason can you give for refusing to turn to God? When you bring the whole thing down to the most basic of principles you must surely see that you have no more reason to be ungodly than to damn your own soul. Either you have a good reason for what you are doing or you do not; and if you do not, are you still determined to go against reason? Will you do something you have no reason for doing? If you think you do have a reason, do the best you can to produce it. What reason can you possibly give for delaying or refusing to respond to God's call? Have you any reason that will satisfy your own conscience, or that you will dare to offer when you stand before God on the Day of Judgement?

Substitutes for sense

Instead of reasons, all that ungodly men have to offer is ignorant nonsense. Here are some of the feeble things that sinners say, and some brief answers to them.

1.   'If only converted, godly men are saved then heaven will be empty.' The person who says this obviously thinks that God does not know what he is saying, or that he is not to be believed. The Bible tells us of multitudes that will be in heaven — even though Jesus made it clear that 'Small is the gate and narrow the road that leads to life, and only a few find it' (Matthew 7:14). Instead of arguing about how many might be saved, the sinner would be better advised to obey Christ's command: 'Enter through the narrow gate' (Matthew 7:13).

2.   'If I go to hell I will have plenty of company.' But will that be any help or comfort to you? Do you think that God will

be put off from executing his righteous judgement because of the numbers of people involved? And do you think that you would have no company in heaven?

3.   'But all men are sinners, even the best of men.' I agree, but not all are unconverted sinners. As we saw in an earlier chapter, true Christians do not live in gross sins, and they constantly long and strive and pray to be rid of all their sins.

4.   'There are many who profess conversion whose lives are no better than those of unbelievers.' Of course there are hypocrites in the church, but true Christians are not like this. There are millions of godly believers whom it would be wicked to charge with hypocrisy. What is more, ungodly men often accuse Christians of hidden sins because they know that these Christians are not guilty of the outward sins which they themselves commit.

5.   'I am not guilty of any gross or vile sins; why do you say I need to be converted?' But you were born with a sinful nature, and you are living to please that sinful nature just like anyone else. Is it not a great sin to love the world more than you love God, and to have a proud, unbelieving heart? Many people who avoid openly disgraceful sins are as glued to the world, as estranged from God, as much slaves to the flesh, and as averse to heaven as those whose lives are grossly offensive.

6.   'But I never harm anyone, nor even mean to; why should God condemn me?' Is it 'no harm' to ignore your Creator and the purpose for which you were created? Is it 'no harm' to neglect the grace that he offers to you every day? If you do not realize this, it is an indication of the depths of your sinfulness. The dead do not feel that they are dead! If you were spiritually

alive you would see just how sinful you are and be amazed that
you could ever have treated the matter so lightly.

7.   'All this talk about eternal things is enough to drive some
people to distraction; it is enough to unbalance people who
think about it too much.' But nobody can be more distracted
or unbalanced than those who neglect their everlasting welfare. Nobody is truly balanced in his mind until he is converted. The Bible says that 'The foolishness of God is wiser
than man's wisdom' (1 Corinthians 1:25) and that 'The fear of
the Lord is the beginning of wisdom' (Psalm 111:10). In the
well-known parable Jesus told, the prodigal son decided to
return to his father 'when he came to his senses' (Luke 15:17).
It is ridiculous to argue that men will disobey God and run into
hell for fear of being driven out of their wits! What would do
this? Would loving God, or calling on him, or forsaking sin, or
loving God's people, or delighting yourself in God's service,
or looking forward to heaven? Are these things that would
drive you mad? And why would God encourage man to think
seriously about these things if they would drive him insane? If
heaven is too high for you to think about and prepare for, it will
be too high for you ever to enter and enjoy. If anyone is
distracted by thinking of eternal things it is because he misun-
derstands them, and it is almost better to be in that state than
to be deluded into thinking that ignoring them is wisdom.

8.   'Does God really care what men speak or think or do? Is
it really that important to him?' The Bible teaches that these
things are important to God, and your common sense ought to
tell you the same thing. Would a sensible man build anything
for no reason? Would you make or buy a watch or a clock and
not care whether it kept good time? Then would God have
created, preserved and upheld you and provided all your daily

needs and not care how you lived? If you do not believe in a God who upholds and provides for you, you certainly cannot believe in a God who can help you when you are in need or in trouble. If God cared nothing for you, you would not still be here; any one of a hundred diseases would have been allowed to end your life. God obviously made man to bring glory to his name; how can you possibly imagine that he does not care whether or not his purposes are fulfilled? Did God have no purpose in creating the world? Why does the earth sustain us all? Did God create all of this, set man in such an honoured place in it all, and then not care how man thinks, speaks or lives? Nothing could be more unreasonable!

9.   'The world was a better place when man did not think religion was so important.' It has always been popular to speak about 'the good old days', but that kind of thinking is usually misguided. Things were never as good as we think or imagine. Of course those who want no religion are bound to think that the world would be a better place without it, but the devil thinks the same way! The fact is that society is at its best when God is most loved, obeyed and served. What other way could you decide whether the world was good or bad?

10.   'There are so many different religions that I have no idea which is right, so I will stay as I am.' But if one religion is right, having no religion is bound to be wrong! Nobody is further off course than worldly, carnal, unconverted sinners, because the whole drift of their lives is wrong. If you were making a journey on which your life depended, would you stop or turn back because you came to a crossroads, or because not everyone was using the same means of transport, or because some got lost? Surely you would want to be all the more certain that you were on the right road? If some of your employees had

difficulty in knowing how to do a certain job, and others wasted time, would you excuse anyone who sat around doing nothing all day?

11.   'I know some Christians who are as poor and who have as many problems as others who are not Christians.' That may be true — and in fact some Christians may be poorer and have more problems than unbelievers, if God sees this would be best for them. But Christians do not treat earthly prosperity or comfort as either their right or their reward; instead, their treasures and hopes are in heaven, and they are content to wait for all the glory that God has prepared for them there.

12.   'I am satisfied to do as well as I can and hope that God will see me all right in the end.' How can you say, 'I do as well as I can,' when you refuse to turn to God, when your heart is set against his holy name and his holy service? You are not doing as well as you can, but only as well as you will. And what can you hope for as a result? If you hope to be saved without being converted and living a holy life, your hope is not in God but in Satan or self. God has made you no such promise.

The longer view

If these arguments and others like them are all you have against conversion and a holy life, they amount to less than nothing. If they will persuade you to turn your back on God and fling yourself into hell, I can only pray that the Lord will deliver you from such spiritual blindness and hardness of heart. Will you dare stand before God with such arguments on the Day of Judgement? Will it do you any good then to say, 'Lord I did not turn to you because I was so busy doing other things, I knew some people who were hypocrites and there were so many different opinions about religious subjects'? What good will that do you? The Bible tells you to 'seek first [God's] kingdom and his righteousness' (Matthew 6:33) and that 'Godliness has value for all things, holding promise for both the present life and the life to come' (1 Timothy 4:8). Then why do you refuse to take any notice? If you are hindered by hypocrites, surely you should be more careful, and not more careless? God tells you to look to the Bible, not to them. Are you confused by so many religious opinions? Then why do you not rely on the Bible, where God's teaching about the way of salvation is perfectly plain?

If these answers will not silence you then God has other things that will. Jesus told a parable about a man who gatecrashed a royal wedding reception but was not properly dressed for the occasion. When the king asked him, 'Friend, how did you get in here without wedding clothes?' the man was 'speechless' (Matthew 22:12) and was thrown out. In the same way, anybody who imagines that he can get to heaven without being converted will be rendered speechless at the Day of Judgement. He will have nothing to say, because he will have no reason to give why he should not have turned to the Lord while he had the opportunity of doing so.

Is your own conscience satisfied with the reasons you give for not turning to God? If it is, you are obviously not serious about repenting. What reasons can you give for staying as you are? Are you determined to go to hell in spite of reason? Think seriously about this while you have time to do so. Can you find any fault with God, or his work, or his promises? Is he a bad master, or is the devil a better one? Is there any harm in a holy life, or is a life of worldliness and ungodliness better? Does your conscience tell you that it would do you any harm to be converted and live a holy life? Would it be harmful if the Spirit of Christ changed your heart? If it is bad to be holy, why does God say, 'Be holy, because I am holy'? (1 Peter 1:16). At the creation God made man 'in his own image' (Genesis 1:27) and it is this image, lost when man fell into sin, that he wants to restore to you. You may be reluctant to live a holy life, but be honest: would you not rather die as one who had? Would you not rather die converted than unconverted, holy than unholy? Is there nothing within you that cries, 'Let me die the death of the righteous, and may my end be like theirs'? (Numbers 23:10). Then why not turn to God now? The fact of the matter is that you will either be converted or wish you had been when it is too late.

What are you afraid of losing if you become a Christian? Your friends? But you will gain new ones. God will be your friend, Christ will be your friend, the Holy Spirit will be your friend, every other Christian in the world will be your friend. The friends you now have will entice you on the way to hell; the Lord Jesus Christ, your new friend, would save you from hell and take you to heaven. Are you afraid of losing your pleasures? Do you imagine that you could never have another happy day if you were converted? How tragic that you should take more pleasure in the things which pander to your sinful nature than in those things which serve God's glory! The Bible says, 'For the kingdom of God is not a matter of eating and drinking, but of righteousness, peace and joy in the Holy Spirit' (Romans 14:17). A child playing with its toys thinks more of them than of any riches you would offer it, and it is foolish wickedness which makes the sinner prefer earthly pleasures and possessions to the riches of the kingdom of God. What will you do when your earthly pleasures and possessions are gone? For the Christian, that is when his greatest joys begin! I know something of what it is like to give myself to earthly pleasures, but I also know the joy of knowing the love of God in Christ — and there is no comparison. There is more joy to be had in one day with Christ than in a lifetime without him. That is why the psalmist says to God,

'Better is one day in your courts
    than a thousand elsewhere;
I would rather be a doorkeeper in the house of my God
    than dwell in the tents of wickedness'
(Psalm 84:10).

It is worth recalling some words written by King Solomon, one of the wealthiest men in history: 'I tried cheering myself with wine, and embracing folly — my mind still guiding me with wisdom. I wanted to see what was worth while for men to do under heaven during the few days of their lives ...

I denied myself nothing my eyes desired;
    I refused my heart no pleasure.
My heart took delight in all my work,
    and this was the reward for all my labour.
Yet when I surveyed all that my hands had done
    and what I had toiled to achieve,
everything was meaningless, a chasing after the wind;
    nothing was gained under the sun'
(Ecclesiastes 2:3, 10-11).

Later on he added,

'Sorrow is better than laughter,
    because a sad face is good for the heart.
The heart of the wise is in the house of mourning,
    but the heart of fools is in the house of pleasure.
It is better to heed a wise man's rebuke
    than to listen to the song of fools.

> Like the crackling of thorns under the pot,
>   so is the laughter of fools.
> This too is meaningless'
>
>   (Ecclesiastes 7:2-6).

The loudest laughter of an unconverted sinner is like that of a man who is tickled — he laughs when he has no cause for joy. Does this make any sense? It is your sinful nature that makes a carnal life seem so pleasant and a holy life so unpleasant; but if you are converted God will give you a new heart, so that it will be more pleasant to get rid of sin than it now is to keep it. You will discover that the only life that satisfies is a life lived for God.

Reasons for unreason

Then why are men so unreasonable when it comes to salvation, yet are perfectly reasonable when considering other things? Why are they so reluctant to be converted that they need so much persuasion, and that even then most will live and die unconverted? Here are six answers to that question.

1. Because man is a sinner by birth, which means that by nature he is in love with the world and with sin and opposed to God and to goodness.

2. Man is in spiritual darkness. He is like a man born blind, who cannot understand a description of 'light'. So the sinner knows nothing about God, the power of the cross of Christ, or the person and work of the Holy Spirit. He cannot understand what it is to be converted, to live a godly life, and to know the certainty of going to heaven. He is in a mist of ignorance, lost

and bewildered in sin, like someone stumbling along at dead of night and not knowing where he is until daylight dawns.

3. They are sure they have no need to be converted, but think that a little bit of moral improvement will be enough to get them to heaven, and nobody who refuses to believe he is lost will take any notice of anyone who tries to point him in the right direction.

4. They have become slaves to their own sinful natures. Their selfish desires and appetites have such a grip on them that they can think of nothing else but satisfying them. But their determination has become their weakness, so that although they say they have no power to turn from sin, the fact is that they have no wish to do so. The sinner is so taken up with earthly things that he has neither heart nor time nor mind for heavenly things.

5. Some are surrounded by so many godless friends that they never give a thought to living a holy life. When one of these friends dies they never imagine for a moment that they have gone to hell, so they are perfectly happy to go on living as their friends had lived and dying as they died. The story is told of a man who was one day driving a flock of lambs over a bridge across the River Severn when something blocked their way. One of the lambs jumped on to the wall of the bridge, but its legs slipped under it and it fell into the river. Before the shepherd could stop them, one lamb after another did the same thing and in a few moments they were drowned. Those behind had no idea of what had happened to those in front, and thought they were safe to follow them, but when they were over the wall they were lost. It is the same with ungodly men who keep ungodly company. One dies and falls into hell, and the others follow without knowing where they are going. When they are

over the wall, and death opens their eyes, they would give anything to be back where they were before!

6.   They have a subtle, powerful and malicious enemy, the devil, whose main aim is to prevent their conversion. He persuades them not to bother with these matters and not to believe the Scriptures. He tells them that a holy life is a miserable life, that there is no need to be converted, and that a God of love will never send anyone to hell, and if they begin to think seriously about their condition he tells them that there is no hurry to do anything about it. By all these deceitful means, the devil keeps most men in his grip and leads them to destruction.

These are some of the reasons why so many people remain unconverted when God has done so much, Christ has suffered so much, and true preachers of the gospel have said so much to bring about their conversion. Even when all their 'reasons' have been explained as worthless, they refuse to listen to God's gracious invitation, 'Turn and live.' As we have now seen the reasonableness of God's commands and the un-reasonableness of man's disobedience, there is only one last major matter to consider: who is at fault if sinners are damned?

8.
The guilty fool

At this point in our examination of God's message to Ezekiel, we have established beyond all doubt that God has done everything he possibly could to save sinners from the folly and fatality of their sin. This leaves us one final principle to consider: *if after all this the wicked refuse to turn, it is not God's fault if they perish; it is theirs. Their own wilfulness is the cause of their own damnation; they are damned because they choose to be.*

One thing is very clear from all we have seen, and that is that if anyone is eternally lost, God is not to blame. In the Old Testament, God pictures mankind as a vineyard which he has planted and tended with great care, only to find that its fruit is poor and sour. As a result he asks, 'What more could have been done for my vineyard than I have done for it?' (Isaiah 5:4). God created man in his own image, gave him reason and understanding, supplied all his needs and gave him his perfect law. When man broke that law God had pity on him and sent his Son to die in the place of sinners; Christ now offers all men the forgiveness of sins and eternal life if they will turn to him in repentance and faith; and the Holy Spirit has enabled generations of faithful preachers to call sinners to turn to God. Can you not see where you fit into that picture? God has sustained your life in the midst of your sins, surrounded you with his mercies every day, and mixed his mercies with afflictions to remind you of your folly and to call you to your senses. In all of this the Holy Spirit has been calling to you, 'Turn to God. Do you know where you are going, or what you are doing? When will you come to your senses, leave your sin and be saved?' To you and to all sinners he pleads, 'Today, if you hear his voice, do not harden your hearts' (Hebrews 3:7).

God sets eternal life before you. He assures you of the certainty of heaven, with all its joy and of hell with all its misery. Other than seeing these things with your own eyes, what more could you ask? In the gospel Jesus Christ has been 'clearly portrayed as crucified' (Galatians 3:1) and you have been told that unless you trust in him you are lost in your sins. You have been told of the sinfulness and emptiness of sin and the worthlessness of all the world's pleasure and wealth. You have been reminded of the brevity and uncertainty of your life and told of the endless duration of the joy or torment that will follow in the life to come. You may even have heard these things so often that you are tired of hearing them. You may be in such a condition that you no longer take any notice of them, like a blacksmith's dog which is so used to the noise of the hammer that it falls asleep even when the sparks fly about its ears. Yet still God offers you mercy if you will turn to him with all your heart.

Who is to blame?

Then in the name of reason you be the judge as to whether it is God's fault or yours that you are still unconverted. If you

remain unsaved it is because you choose to. What more could
be said or done to you that would be more likely to change your
mind? Can you honestly say, 'I would gladly turn to God but
I am not able to; I would gladly forsake my sin but I am not able
to; I would gladly change the way I think, speak and act but I
am not able to?' Why not? It is the wickedness of your own
heart that prevents you. Who forces you to sin? You have the
same time and liberty and opportunity to live a godly life as
anyone else — then why are you not doing so? Have church
doors been locked against you? Does the Bible exclude you
from its promises of mercy and forgiveness to sinners who turn
to God? Does God forbid you to pray to him? You know the
answers to those questions. It is you yourself who have
determined not to live a godly life, not to go to church, not to
read God's Word, not to pray, not to turn to Christ.

If God had made an exception in your case to his gracious
promise of mercy, or had specifically told you that he would
have nothing to do with you, regardless of how earnestly you
called upon him, you would at least have some excuse for your
condition. But this is not the case. You could long ago have had
Christ to be your Lord and Saviour, but you determined not to
come to him because you did not think you needed to. Jesus
once told a parable in which some people rebelled against the
man who had been appointed as their ruler. They cried out,
'We don't want this man to be our king' (Luke 19:14). In the
same way, sinners reject Christ's right to rule their lives. As we
saw in an earlier chapter, when he went to Jerusalem for the
last time, Jesus wept over its sin and said, 'O Jerusalem,
Jerusalem, you who kill the prophets and stone those sent to
you, how often I have longed to gather your children together,
as a hen gathers her chicks under her wings, but you were not
willing' (Matthew 23:37). God said the same kind of thing in
Old Testament days: 'Oh, that their hearts would be inclined

to fear me and keep all my commands always, so that it might
go well with them and their children for ever!' (Deuteronomy
5:29); 'If only they were wise and would understand this and
discern what their end will be!' (Deuteronomy 32:29). But we
are also told what God does when people reject him:

'But my people would not listen to me;
    Israel would not submit to me.
So I gave them over to their stubborn hearts
    to follow their own devices'

(Psalm 81:11-12).

'Your wickedness will punish you;
    your backsliding will rebuke you.
Consider then and realize
    how evil and bitter it is for you
when you forsake the Lord your God
    and have no awe of me'

(Jeremiah 2:19).

So now, God condescends to reason with you. He puts his
case to you. He asks, 'What is there about me or about serving
me that you hate so much? What harm have I done to you?
Have I deserved this kind of treatment? Is it I or Satan who is
your enemy? Is it I or self that would ruin you? Is it a holy life
or a life of sin that you should run away from? If you are lost
it is because you would not turn to me and be saved.'

Invitation and warning

But God does not want you to be lost, so once again he calls
you to consider your ways and turn to him:

'Come, all you who are thirsty,
     come to the waters;
and you who have no money,
     come, buy and eat!
Come, buy wine and milk
     without money and without cost.
Why spend money on what is not bread,
     and your labour on what does not satisfy?
Listen, listen to me, and eat what is good,
     and your soul will delight in the richest of fare.
Give ear and come to me;
     hear me, that your soul may live...
Seek the Lord while he may be found;
     call upon him while he is near.
Let the wicked forsake his way
     and the evil man his thoughts.
Let him turn to the Lord, and he will have mercy on him,
     and to our God, for he will freely pardon'
                                        (Isaiah 55:1-3, 6-7).

But God has something equally clear to say to those who
reject such an amazing invitation:

'Be appalled at this, O heavens,
     and shudder with great horror...
My people have committed two sins:
They have forsaken me,
     the spring of living water,
and have dug their own cisterns,
     broken cisterns that cannot hold water'
                                        (Jeremiah 2:12-13).

Is this not exactly what you have done? Time and again
Christ has given you his wonderful invitation: 'Whoever is

thirsty, let him come; and whoever wishes, let him take the free
gift of the water of life' (Revelation 22:17), and your refusal
forces him to say that 'You refuse to come to me to have life'
(John 5:40). He has invited you to feast with him in the
kingdom of his grace, and you have made excuses for not
accepting his invitation. Then you should not be surprised to
hear him say, as the man did in Jesus's parable, 'I tell you, not
one of those men who were invited will get a taste of my
banquet' (Luke 14:24).

In the Old Testament there is a very challenging passage
about this in which 'Wisdom' is used as the equivalent of
God's voice calling people to consider their ways:

'Wisdom calls aloud in the street,
    she raises her voice in the public squares;
at the head of the noisy streets she cries out,
    in the gateways of the city she makes her speech:
"How long will you simple ones love your simple ways?
    How long will mockers delight in mockery
    and fools hate knowledge?
If you had responded to my rebuke,
    I would have poured out my heart to you
    and made my thoughts known to you.
But since you rejected me when I called
    and no one gave heed when I stretched out my hand,
since you ignored all my advice
    and would not accept my rebuke,
I in turn will laugh at your disaster;
    I will mock when calamity overtakes you —
when calamity overtakes you like a storm,
    when disaster sweeps over you like a whirlwind,
    when distress and trouble overwhelm you.

Then they will call to me but I will not answer;
  they will look for me but will not find me.
Since they hated knowledge
  and did not choose to fear the Lord,
since they would not accept my advice
  and spurned my rebuke,
they will eat the fruit of their ways
  and be filled with the fruit of their schemes.
For the waywardness of the simple will kill them,
  and the complacency of fools will destroy them;
but whoever listens to me will live in safety
  and be at ease, without fear of harm"'

(Proverbs 1:20-33).

Notice how clearly those words show that the wicked are destroyed not because God did not teach them, but because they would not hear; not because God did not call them, but because they would not turn to him. It is sheer blasphemy to blame God for the sinner's destruction. What is more, those who blame God are totally unqualified to do so. They say that God is harsh in condemning all the unconverted, they think it unfair to punish temporary sins with everlasting destruction, and they say that they can do nothing about it; yet all the time they are busy destroying themselves and nothing will persuade them to stop. They think that God is cruel in condemning them, whereas it is they who are being cruel to themselves by deliberately running headlong into hell and taking no notice of God's promises or warnings. Their lifestyle tells us that they are under the devil's control; if they die as they are, nothing in the world can save them. Their lives hang by a thread, yet when we warn them of their danger and plead with them to have pity on their own souls, they refuse to listen. When we urge them to turn from their sins and put their trust in Christ, they will

have none of it; yet they say that God is cruel to condemn them!
But it is not God who is cruel. God is not cruel to you; he tells
you to turn or burn — and you will not turn. He tells you that
if you keep your sins you must have his judgement to go with
them — and you are determined to keep them. He tells you that
the only way to be happy is to be holy — and you refuse to be
holy. What more can God say or do? You are in a swamp of sin
and misery and God offers to lift you out. He says, 'All day
long I have held out my hands to a disobedient and obstinate
people' (Romans 10:21), and you refuse his offer; you love
your sins and will not let them go. Are you suggesting that God
should take you to heaven against your will, or take you and
your sins to heaven together? You might as well expect him to
turn the sun to darkness: 'For what do righteousness and
wickedness have in common? Or what fellowship can light
have with darkness?' (2 Corinthians 6:14). The Bible is
perfectly clear about the qualifications for going to heaven:
'Nothing impure will ever enter it, nor will anyone who does
what is shameful or deceitful' (Revelation 21:27).

The fact is that obstinate sinners will neither cry to God for
mercy nor have mercy on themselves. The drunkard is told that
he is poisoning himself on the way to hell, and he says he
cannot help it. The careless worldling is told that if he goes on
living as he is he will never get to heaven, and he does nothing
about it. If we beg sinners to turn for the sake of God who made
them, for the sake of Christ who died for them and for the sake
of their own souls, to have pity on themselves and go no further
on the road to hell, but instead to come to Christ while his arms
are open, the door to everlasting life stands open and mercy is
freely offered to them, they refuse to be persuaded. All they
will say is, 'I hope that somehow God will have mercy on me.'
But if they will not turn to him there is no possibility of mercy.
The Bible specifically says of them,

'For this is a people without understanding;
so their Maker has no compassion on them,
and their Creator shows them no favour'
(Isaiah 27:11).

Blaming God

If someone should refuse to help you when you were without food or clothing, or ill-treated you in some other way, you would say that he was being unmerciful, yet by deliberately casting away your own body and soul you are being a thousand times more unmerciful to yourself. What is more, unless God allows you to spit in his Son's face by ignoring all that he did in dying for sinners, shut your ears to the voice of the Holy Spirit, treat sin as a joke and make a mockery of holiness, and then save you in spite of your refusal of his offer of forgiveness, you dare to say that he is not a God of love! If you were as careful to avoid sin and its consequences as you are to find excuses for your behaviour and to put the blame on God, you would be better employed. It is frightening to think that men have such a high opinion of themselves that in looking for excuses they are prepared to blame God for their predicament. That is what happened when Adam first ate the forbidden fruit in the Garden of Eden. He told God, 'The woman you put here with me — she gave me some fruit from the tree, and I ate it' (Genesis 3:12) — implying that at least indirectly God was the culprit. So today men say to God, 'It was the understanding you gave me that was unable to discern the truth; it was the will you gave me that made the wrong choice; it was you who allowed me to be tempted; it was you who put all these sinful things in my way.' This kind of twisted thinking is the sinner's trademark. Because he instinctively knows that God is the cause of everything that is good, he assumes that he must also be the cause of everything that is evil. He tries to make his own decisions, but when things go wrong he tries to shift the blame on to God.

Let me deal with two objections that people raise at this point.

Firstly, there are those who say, 'But surely we cannot convert ourselves until God converts us? Surely Scripture teaches that "It does not ... depend on man's desire or effort, but on God's mercy"?' (Romans 9:16). Yes it does, but we need to understand that there is a difference between mercy and salvation. If a man is to be saved there must be both 'desire' (willingness) and 'effort', and God promises salvation only to those who have the desire and make the effort. On the other hand, it is God's mercy that produces both the willingness and the effort. This does not mean that when a man is willing, and strives to be saved, his willingness and striving deserve to be rewarded, but it does mean that the sinner's deliberate refusal to accept God's mercy means that he can never be saved. The sinner's greatest disability is his stubborn unwillingness, which makes his sin even greater. He would be able to turn if he was willing to do so; but his will is so corrupted that nothing but God's sovereign grace can change it. So he has all the more reason to ask for God's grace, do everything he can to hear about it and yield to everything he discovers of it; and he has no reason at all to neglect it and set himself against it. Let him do everything he is able to do, and then blame God if he can!

Secondly, there are those who say, 'But where does man's free will come into the picture?' The argument about free will is not something that sinners can properly understand and I will therefore keep to one simple point about it. To talk of a man as having a will that is 'free' is not strictly true, or is at least misleading. Man's will is 'free' in the sense that it is a self-determining faculty, yet it is not strictly 'free' because by nature it is fatally biased towards evil. Man's will is in bondage to his sinful nature, but this does not mean that his will is morally 'neutral' or innocent. If someone maliciously wounded you, or stole some of your property, or killed one of your children, would you excuse him if he protested, 'But I have no free will, my sinful nature is to blame'? If that were the case, every criminal could plead the same excuse and expect to be acquitted. But if that would not be a good enough excuse in those cases, neither is it any excuse for you to say that you have no choice in the matter of sin.

What a subtle tempter the devil is! What a deceitful thing sin is! What a foolish, corrupted creature man is! The devil must certainly be subtle if he can persuade most men to walk straight into everlasting fire when they have received so many warnings. Sin must certainly be deceitful if it can fool millions into forfeiting everlasting life for something so vile. And man must certainly be foolish and corrupted if he can so easily be cheated of so much for the sake of something that amounts to nothing. You would think it impossible that anyone would be so stupid as to throw himself into fire or water, yet sinners are perfectly happy to throw themselves into hell. If it were impossible for you to die until you decided to end your life, how long would you choose to live? Yet when, under God's grace, everlasting life is in your own hands, in the sense that it is yours as long as you refuse to throw it away, how foolish it is to do so! What is more, sinners are so inclined to evil that they not only destroy themselves, they do not hesitate to drag others down with them.

Man's worst enemy

All of this tells us that man is his own worst enemy, and the worst thing that can happen to him in this life is to be left to himself. Man's greatest complaint should be against himself; his greatest work is to resist his own sinful nature; his greatest concern should be to pray and strive against the blindness, corruption, perversion and wickedness that spring from his own sinful heart; and the greatest thing that the grace of God has to do is to save us from ourselves. This being the case, I must ask you to judge from the evidence. If you do, you will surely be driven to the conclusion that you are guilty before God, guilty of your own destruction. Here are some further points which I hope will help to convince you, humble you and lead you to take the right action.

1. You have no reason for believing that God is cruel or is in any way to blame for your destruction, because the Bible clearly teaches that that is not in accordance with his nature:

> 'The Lord is righteous in all his ways
>   and loving towards all he has made...
> He fulfils the desires of those who fear him;
>   he hears their cry and saves them'
>
> (Psalm 145:17,19).

On the other hand, we know that man's understanding is darkened, his will corrupt and his affections polluted. He is therefore well qualified to destroy himself. If you came across a wolf and a sheep standing near a dead lamb, which one would you suspect of being the killer? If a murder was committed, would you suspect someone known for his integrity, or a known assassin? And the Bible says, 'When tempted, no one should say, "God is tempting me." For God cannot be tempted by evil, nor does he tempt anyone; but each one is tempted when, by his own evil desire, he is dragged away and enticed. Then, after desire has conceived, it gives birth to sin; and sin, when it is full-grown, gives birth to death' (James 1:13-15). Sin is the result of man's sinfulness; there is no way in which God can be blamed. Man is like a poisonous spider being entangled and killed by its own efforts.

2. You can see that you are guilty of your own destruction by noticing how ready you are to yield to temptation. You are as ready to yield as the devil is to tempt. If he tempts you to sinful thoughts, or words, or actions, you are ready to give in. If he wants to keep you from holy thoughts, or good resolutions, or pure words, or generous actions, he needs no encouragement. You are ready to meet him halfway and to go along with anything he suggests. You are hardly ever prepared to resist him, fight him or quench the sparks of sin he tries to kindle.

3. Your guilt can be seen by the way in which you resist all attempts to save you. God points you to his Word and you resist it. The Holy Spirit speaks to you and you shut your ears. A Christian friend rebukes your sin and you are angry at him. He tries to bring you under the sound of the gospel and you put him off with some excuse, or tell him you will manage without it. If someone tries to engage you in serious conversation about your spiritual condition, you find one way or another of wriggling out of it. You are so wise in your own eyes that you simply will not listen to anyone who tries to convince you of biblical truth.

4. You are seen to be guilty by the way in which you are opposed to the truth about God. You think God's wisdom is unfair and his justice cruel. You think he treats sinners as lightly as you do. You imagine that his threatenings are false, and you are prepared to presume upon his goodness and to continue in sin in the hope that somehow or other God will find a way to save you.

5. You destroy yourself by imagining in some vague way that because Christ died for sinners, and you are a sinner, then you are bound to be saved. You imagine that even if you refuse to trust him as your Saviour and submit to him as your Lord, you will somehow be saved by his death and resurrection. But this is not the case! The Bible makes it clear that those whose lives have not been changed have never been converted, and that those who truly trust in Christ are transformed; it speaks of 'our great God and Saviour, Jesus Christ, who gave himself for us to redeem us from all wickedness and to purify for himself a people that are his very own, eager to do what is good' (Titus 2:13-14).

6. Your guilt can be seen in the way in which you misuse God's dealings with you. Perhaps you are one of those who say that if God predestines some people to salvation, and you are not among them, then you are not to blame for your condition, and so you carry on living a godless life. Or if your life is afflicted in some way you blame God. On the other hand, if you prosper you tend to forget God and ignore eternal issues, and if other ungodly friends prosper it convinces you all the more that there is no point in becoming a Christian. Who is to blame for all of this?

7. You take for granted God's goodness to you, and use the blessings he grants you as instruments of disobedience. You eat and drink to satisfy your own appetites, not to enable you to serve your Maker. The clothes you wear are used to bolster your pride; wealth draws your attention away from heaven; if men praise you it puffs you up; if you have health and strength, you forget that life is very short; if other men succeed, you envy them and covet what they have; even beauty becomes an object of lust.

8. The very gifts and abilities that God has given you lead you into sin. If you are greatly gifted you grow proud and self-conceited; if you are less gifted you complain. You may have an element of religion in your life, but even that is corrupted; your prayers are ruined because you do not 'turn away from wickedness' (2 Timothy 2:19); you may read the Bible occasionally but because you turn 'a deaf ear to the law' your prayers are 'detestable' (Proverbs 28:9). Listen to what God says to you: 'Guard your steps when you go to the house of God. Go near to listen rather than to offer the sacrifice of fools, who do not know that they do wrong' (Ecclesiastes 5:1).

9. You even turn the common actions of other people into opportunities to sin. If they are godly you hate them; if they are ungodly you imitate them. If most of your friends are ungodly you feel safe in their company; if you know only a few Christians you feel comfortable in despising them. If a Christian seems particularly holy in his life you think he is being too meticulous; if one falls into sin you feel justified in doing the same. If one is found to be a hypocrite, you say, 'I always suspected that Christians were like that,' and you imagine that you are as good as any of them. Even a small slip is enough to make you feel justified in sinning; a Christian cuts his finger and you are happy to cut your throat! If there is a scandal in a church you tar every church with the same brush. If someone tries to stop you believing heresy you hold on to it for dear life. If you hear of Christians disagreeing on some point of doctrine you refuse to listen to the basic doctrines on which they all agree.

The stupidity of self-destruction

In these and other ways it is difficult not to come to the conclusion that sinners are destroying themselves. Are you not

prepared to admit that some or all of these things are true about
you? If not, consider the following points.

1. To destroy yourself is to sin against the first principle in
your nature, that of self-preservation. When Jesus said you
should 'love your neighbour as yourself' (Matthew 19:19) the
inference is that you quite properly love yourself, but if you
love yourself so little that you are prepared to throw yourself
into hell, one assumes that you would be prepared to drag the
whole world with you.

2. By living to gratify your own selfish desires you are doing
yourself the worst possible harm. If you really want lasting
pleasure, endless riches and eternal honour it is the height of
foolishness to look for them on the road to hell.

3. What a tragedy it is that you are doing to yourself something which no one else on earth or in hell can do to you! If all
the world were against you, and every devil in hell joined in,
they could not force you to sin or to destroy yourself without
your consent. Yet you know that the devil is your enemy and
longs for your destruction; then why do something that not
even all the devils in hell can do to you? When you deliberately
sin, when you turn away from godliness, when you reject
God's call, you are hurting yourself in the worst way possible
and doing something that not even the worst of men and devils
can do.

4. You are betraying a sacred trust which God has given you.
God says, 'Above all else, guard your heart, for it is the
wellspring of life' (Proverbs 4:23), but by your careless living
you are betraying that trust.

5. By refusing to listen to those who try to help you, you make it all the more certain that on the Day of Judgement God will refuse your cry for help. He will be perfectly justified in turning you away because when the opportunity was yours you would not have pity on yourself nor listen to those who wanted to help you.

6. It will be terrible beyond words to remember in hell that you brought all of this upon yourself. It will torture you for ever to remember that you were warned again and again, that you sinned with a clear understanding of what you were doing, that you repeatedly and deliberately shut your ears to God's voice, that you took no notice of Christian friends and that you refused Christ's offer of forgiveness — and all for the sake of earthly pleasures and self-satisfaction! The Bible says, 'Of what use is money in the hand of a fool, since he has no desire to get wisdom?' (Proverbs 17:16), and it will be painful to remember that you had the means of obtaining eternal life, but were not prepared to pay the price of turning from your sin. God's Word to you remains the same:

'Listen to my instruction and be wise;
    do not ignore it.
Blessed is the man who listens to me;
    watching daily at my doors,
    waiting at my doorway.
For whoever finds me finds life
    and receives favour from the Lord.
But whoever fails to find me harms himself;
    all who hate me love death'
                                    (Proverbs 8:33-36).

9.
Invitation to live

My work is nearly finished, and I am heavy-hearted to think that after all I have written, the world, the flesh and the devil may have such a hold on you that you will remain just as you were when you began reading this book. If that should be the case, God knows that I can say with one of the Old Testament prophets, 'I have not desired the day of despair' (Jeremiah 17:16). It would break my heart to know that all my work had been in vain, I am so afraid that you may be shut out of heaven and shut up in hell that I must ask you once again, what are you going to do? Will you turn or will you die? I feel like a doctor telling a dangerously ill patient that the only way he will survive is to change his lifestyle and take the prescribed medication. What would you think of someone who refused such advice? Yet you are in exactly that kind of position. But if you will turn from your sin and trust in Christ you will have eternal life. And we are not dealing with just physical illness. If that were the case, you could be physically restrained from doing yourself harm. If necessary, the medicine that would save your life could be forced down your throat. But the same kind of thing is not true about soul-sickness. You cannot be saved against your will or be dragged to heaven in a strait-jacket. In his wisdom, God has ordained that man's will has a crucially important part to play in his salvation; no one goes to heaven or hell against his will. Instead, in either heaven or hell he will have to say, 'I chose to be here.'

The need to be willing

If only you were sincerely and wholeheartedly willing! How tragic that men who are so foolish and react so negatively in such an important matter can be so sensible and courteous in smaller things! As far as I know, most of the people who live around me would be glad to do me any reasonable favour they could; yet when I ask the greatest thing in the world (and not for me but for them), the most that many of them will give me is a patient hearing. There are many people who treat preaching like that; they seem to doubt whether the preacher is being serious. If I warned people of a quicksand, or some other danger, they would take notice; but when they are warned that the devil is lying in wait for them, that sin is poisoning them and that hell is not to be trifled with, they go on as if they had not heard a word.

But the subject *is* serious and I write these words in deadly earnest. I would hope that if my life was at stake and you had the means to save me, you would do so. If I was in desperate need of a drink of water, or a bite of food, or a few clothes to keep me from freezing to death, would you not give them to me? Then look upon me now as a beggar, but one who is pleading not for my life to be saved, but yours — and not just your body but your soul. I plead with you now, as if I were on my knees before you, that you would listen to God's voice, turn to Christ and be saved. However ignorant or careless or steeped in sin you may have been, however many times you may have ignored him in the past, I beg of you not to go one day longer in your lost condition, but to call upon God to give you his grace and to make you a new creature, so that you may escape the horrors of hell. If you would grant me anything, grant me this, that you will turn from your sinful ways and live. Deny me anything, as long as you grant me this, because if you deny me this there is nothing else you could grant me in its place. If you would do anything for the One who created you and who died that sinners might live, then do not deny him this, because if you do, there is nothing else you can give him. Just as you would want him to hear your prayers, grant your requests and meet your need at the moment of your death and at the Day of Judgement, then do not deny him this one request while you have the opportunity. My friend, believe me, death and judgement, heaven and hell are very different matters when you come close to them than they seem to be when you think they are at a distance!

The way of salvation

I have nearly finished, and I hope with all my heart that some who have read these words will by now be conscious of their need and want to be converted, like the man in the New Testament who cried out to the apostles, 'Sirs, what must I do to be saved?' (Acts 16:30). If that is your position, if you are seriously asking, 'How can I be converted? I need to be saved, I want to be saved but I need to know exactly what I must do,' then for the last time let me remind you of your condition and give you some clear and straightforward directions.

Firstly, you need to understand the need and nature of true conversion. Until you are converted you are under the guilt of all the sins you have ever committed, and under the wrath of God and the curse of his holy law. You are a servant of the devil, working for him against God, yourself and everyone else. You are spiritually dead and morally deformed and know nothing of God or of the holiness he requires. You are unable to please God in anything you do. You have no promise of his help and are in daily danger of his justice, not knowing when you might be snatched into eternity. You will certainly be lost for ever in hell if you die in your present condition. No amount of respectability or moral improvement can save you. Only true conversion, producing a new heart and a new life, can prevent your being lost for ever.

Signs of life

What will be the results of your conversion? In the first place you will immediately become one of the 'members of God's household' (Ephesians 2:19). You will receive a new life, which will go on 'being renewed in knowledge in the image of its Creator' (Colossians 3:10). The Lord Jesus Christ will be your own personal Saviour. You will be saved from the tyranny of Satan, the dominion of sin and the judgement of God's law. All your sins will be forgiven. You will be accepted by God as one of his children, and have liberty to come freely to him in prayer in every situation, knowing that he is willing to hear you. The Holy Spirit will live within you, teaching you the meaning of Scripture, guiding you in your daily life and helping you to be holy. You will become part of the fellowship of all Christian believers. You will be eligible and able to serve God and therefore to be a means of help to many other people.

You will have everything that is truly good for you, and be given grace to bear any afflictions that God in his wisdom allows. You will know something of what it is to have a living relationship with God the Holy Spirit, especially in Bible reading and prayer, and in public worship, where your soul will be fed on the Word of God. You will join those who, though still living on earth, are 'heirs of God and joint heirs with Christ' (Romans 8:17, NKJV), and you will be able to live and die in peace because by faith you will already see the certainty of the everlasting glory that awaits you in heaven.

These are some of the blessings that will be yours in this life, and there will be even greater blessings in heaven. When you die your soul will immediately be 'with Christ, which is far better' (Philippians 1:23, NKJV), and at the Day of Judgement your reunited soul and body will be justified and glorified, so that you will enter into the fulness of the eternal joy which God has prepared for you. In heaven your mortal body will be made immortal, that which was 'perishable' will be 'imperishable' and that which was 'sown in dishonour' will be 'raised in glory' (1 Corinthians 15:42-43). You will never again experience hunger, thirst, tiredness, sickness, sin, shame, sorrow or death. You will be perfectly and finally free from all of these, and perfectly fitted for the knowledge, love and worship of God. With all others in heaven, you will see the indescribable glory of God and be able to love him perfectly and worship him for ever. Your own glory will contribute to heaven's glory; it will not be something private and selfish. What is more, your glory will contribute to the glorifying of your Saviour, Jesus Christ, who will know that your glory was brought about by 'the suffering of his soul' and 'be satisfied' (Isaiah 53:11). And God the Father will be glorified in your glory, not only by receiving your worship, but by seeing the completion of his glorious work of salvation in you, and by

sharing his glory with you. Even the poorest and weakest of
Christians will enjoy all of these things for ever.

But you must remember that none of these blessings can be
yours unless you are truly converted; and to be truly converted
means to turn with all your heart from the world, the flesh and
the devil. It means to turn from the world, which is always
trying to trap you, from the flesh (your own carnal self), which
is always demanding to be pleased, and from the devil, who
deceives you into disobeying God. But conversion involves
not only turning *from* but turning *to*. You must turn to God the
Father, who calls you, to the Lord Jesus Christ, who is the only
way to the Father, and to the Holy Spirit, who alone can enable
you to turn. You must turn to the means of grace (the Bible,
prayer and the church) that God has provided for you; and you
must turn to holiness of life. There must be genuine repentance
and faith.

Think — and act!

Secondly, if you want to be converted you must think earnestly
and seriously about the issues involved. Conversion is not
something trivial or superficial. Get alone and think seriously
about why God created you; then think of the life you have
lived, the sins you have committed and the danger you are in.
Think of the brevity of life, think of the certainty of death and
judgement, think of the joys of heaven, and the torments of hell
and the eternity of both. Then think of the love of Christ, of his
suffering and death, and of his glory as the Saviour of men.
Make sure that you thoroughly absorb all of these things in
your heart.

Thirdly, if you are serious about being converted, make
sure that you read the Scriptures, 'which are able to make you

wise for salvation through faith in Christ Jesus' (2 Timothy 3:15), and, if you can, read other Christian books which explain the Bible's teaching, especially with regard to salvation. Make sure that you regularly attend a place of worship, where the Word of God is faithfully preached. God has ordained preaching as one of the principal means of men's conversion. When the apostle Paul was commanded to preach, the Lord told him, 'I have appeared to you to appoint you as a servant and as a witness of what you have seen of me and what I will show you. I will rescue you from your own people and from the Gentiles. I am sending you to them to open their eyes and turn them from darkness to light, and from the power of Satan to God, so that they may receive forgiveness of sins and a place among those who are sanctified by faith in me' (Acts 26:16-18). Later, Paul himself wrote these words: 'Everyone who calls on the name of the Lord will be saved. How, then, can they call on the one they have not believed in? And how can they believe in the one of whom they have not heard? And how can they hear without someone preaching to them?' (Romans 10:13-14).

Fourthly, turn to God in earnest, constant prayer. Confess your sins and ask for his grace to illuminate and convert you. Ask him to forgive you for everything that is past and to give you his Holy Spirit to change your heart and life and to lead you into a life of holiness. Make this your constant prayer.

Fifthly, make a determined effort to forsake every known sin. Seek to hate the sins which once you loved. Do everything you can to turn away from sin in every way, shape or form.

Sixthly, if possible change the kind of company you have been keeping. This does not mean walking out on your family or ignoring your relations, but it does mean being careful to avoid unnecessary sinful companions and relationships. Find Christian friends, meet with them as often as you can, and talk with them about becoming a Christian and living the Christian life.

Seventhly, surrender yourself to Christ as the great Physician of souls. He himself said, 'I am the way and the truth and the life. No one comes to the Father except through me' (John 14:6), and the Bible teaches us that 'Salvation is found in no one else, for there is no other name under heaven given to men by which we must be saved' (Acts 4:12). Read and study all you can about who he is, what he has done to save sinners, and how he is perfectly equipped to meet all your spiritual needs.

No doubting — no delaying

Eighthly, if you are serious about becoming a Christian, then act with urgency. If you are not willing to become a Christian today, you are not willing at all. Remember yet again that if you are still unconverted as you read these words, you are still 'dead in trespasses and sins' (Ephesians 2:1, NKJV), still under God's righteous wrath and on the very brink of death and hell. No sensible person could be at ease in that condition. If you realized what danger you were in, what loss you are suffering and what a safer and better life you might live, you would not hesitate a moment longer. Your life is short and uncertain, and what a disaster it will be if you die before you turn to God! You have already waited too long, wronged God too long, and every day you delay sin is getting stronger, and conversion is becoming more difficult and unlikely. You dare not try to put things off until nearer the end of your life, because God may have forsaken you by then and you will be lost for ever.

Ninthly, if you want to turn to God and live, do it unreservedly, absolutely and totally. Half measures will not do; you cannot divide your heart between Christ and the world, or part with some sins and keep the rest. To try to do so would be to delude yourself. You must be willing to forsake everything if you want to be a true follower of Christ. As he himself put it, 'Any of you who does not give up everything he has cannot be my disciple' (Luke 14:33). If you will not have Christ on those terms, if God and glory are not good enough for you, but you must hold on to earthly things as well, it is useless to think you can be saved. Nor is it enough to become religious. It is possible to be religious and still to be utterly self-centred, with your own pleasure, possessions or comfort as your main aim, but this is as certain a way to be lost as if you were living in open and gross sin.

Finally, if you want to turn to God and live then do it firmly and definitely, and not as if the issues involved were in any doubt. Let there be no wavering, as if you were unsure whether God or your sinful nature would be the better master, or whether sin or holiness is the better way of life, or whether heaven or hell is the better destiny. Instead, let there be a clear break with sin and a clear commitment to Christ. Let there be no changing of your mind from one day to the next; instead, surrender all that you are and have into God's hands. Do it before you sleep another night, before you move from where you are, before the devil has time to deflect you. Now, while you are reading these very words, turn to God and ask him to save you. His promise remains as true today as when he first made it: 'You will seek me *and find me* when you seek me with all your heart' (Jeremiah 29:13).

I have now done all that I can that you might respond to God's command to turn to him and live. I have sown the seed, as God commanded me to. If there was anything else I could do, I would gladly do it, but I can go no further. Only God can open your mind to understand the gospel and open your heart to receive it. Only you can consider God's call and respond to it.

'Gracious Father, who has sworn that you do not delight in the death of the wicked, but rather that they turn from their wickedness and live, bless these persuasions and directions. Do not allow the great deceiver of men's souls to overcome your Son, your Spirit and your Word. Have pity on poor, unconverted sinners who have no heart to pity or help themselves. Command the spiritually blind to see, the spiritually deaf to hear and the spiritually dead to live. Do not allow sin and death to resist you. Awaken the careless, make the undecided decide and the uncertain certain. Cause sinners who read these lines to weep over their sins and come to their senses and to your Son, before their sins bring them to destruction. Speak the word, and may these poor efforts of mine result in the salvation of many, to their everlasting joy and your everlasting glory.'

Postscript

If you have turned to God and become a Christian
through the reading of this book, and would like
help in beginning to read the Bible for yourself,
you are invited to write to John Blanchard, c/o
Evangelical Press, 12 Wooler Street, Darlington,
Co. Durham, DL1 1RQ, England for a free copy of
Read Mark Learn, his book of guidelines for personal
Bible study based on Mark's Gospel.

If you need further help, please contact the
following person:

Also by John Blanchard

Foreword by John F. MacArthur Jr

Will the real

JESUS

please stand up?

JOHN BLANCHARD

'The finest book I have ever read explaining who Jesus really is. Carefully reasoned, rooted in the Bible, and written in a popular easy-to-read style, this book will prove thrilling for the Christian and very convincing to the sceptic or unbeliever.'

'Highly recommended to all those who want to know what are the solid historical foundations for Christianity, as well as what it means for us today. Here, instead of the fuzzy versions of the Christian faith usually served up by the media, are the facts of the matter, splendidly brought together and clearly argued.'

'Behind the lightweight but arresting title the author's careful scholarship is wedded to a thoughtful "explanation" and defence of the biblical doctrine of the person and work of Christ.'

'In this superlative book John Blanchard has greatly increased the debt we already owe him.'